Improv Manifesto

7 Easy Steps to Confidence, Creativity, and Charisma - Even If You're Shy!

(Think On Your Feet Under Pressure: Tools from Improvisational Theater and Improv Comedy.)

Chad Elliot
"The Confidence Doctor"

Disclaimer:
This book is designed to provide information and motivation to our
readers. It is sold with the understanding that the publisher is not
engaged to render any type of psychological, legal, or any other kind of
professional advice. The content is the sole expression and opinion of
its author, and not necessarily that of the publisher. No warranties or
guarantees are expressed or implied by the publisher's choice to include
any of the content in this volume. Neither the publisher nor the author
shall be liable for any physical, psychological, emotional, financial, or
commercial damages, including, but not limited to, special, incidental,
consequential or other damages. Our views and rights are the same:
You are responsible for your own choices, actions, and results.

Table of Contents

Introduction:
The Success Secrets of Famous Actors

Hi, I'm Chad!

Why the hell should you read this book? Who cares about improv anyway? How could something so silly make your life better?

Let's start by defining what we mean by improv, because it's totally different to different people. Some people think of improv only as improv comedy. You've probably seen *Whose Line Is It Anyway?* On the show, you can see adults in fancy suits using each other as wheel barrows, licking each other's faces, and singing songs about the toilet. That, folks, is improv comedy. It's a bunch of games designed to get laughter from jokes and gags. But, that's only one small part of improvisational theater.

Is improvisational theater silly and funny? Sure! It can have people laughing until they cry. Luckily, it can do much more than that. True improvisational theater is one of the most amazing human accomplishments. The improvisers are actors, directors, and writers all rolled into one! Plus, they are co-writing with other people - people they may have never met before in their lives. They don't get to do any editing and there are no do-overs. When you improvise you create everything from scratch. It's done in the moment and you don't know what's going to happen next. It's one of the most intense forms of co-creation, teamwork, and creativity in the world.

In order to do this successfully, you need a number of valuable skills. That's what this book is about. It gives you the skills, tools and strategies to take what might have seemed impossible and put it easily within your grasp. I've seen people who previously never believed they could think on their feet in even casual situations. Those same people can now improvise scenes, stories, and speeches successfully in front of an audience. It's not a matter of talent, it's a matter of knowledge.

Surprisingly, these skills transfer incredibly effectively to real-life. The concepts that make you a fun partner to create with on stage also make you a fun partner in the real-world. The techniques to unleash your creativity in an improv scene work just as well in business. The understandings of human dynamics that allow you to create interesting characters on stage also allow you to redefine who you are. You'll quickly learn they give you greater understanding of the people around you - and, allow you to communicate with them more effectively. You'll discover how the storytelling and body language skills so powerful in the theater are useful for becoming an engaging public speaker. Finally, the confidence, quick-thinking, and awareness you develop in improv is useful anywhere.

Please realize this is two books in one. This is a book on how to improvise successfully on stage, and I'll give clear examples of how to use what you learn in that context. But, that's just the tip of the iceberg. It's also a book on how to live a rewarding life. I'll also give you many examples of how what you're learning applies to public speaking, business, dating, job interviews, and parenting. In other words, how to use it to become happier, more successful, and more at ease in any situation.

The book is divided into 7 chapters. Each chapter embodies one of the 7 simple steps to success improvising. The progression is in a very logical order. We start with the goal of makings sure you're in the present moment, because improvisation is impossible if you're stuck in your head. We then progress to the skills that allow you to make a strong first impression and set yourself up for success. Next is how to unleash your creativity and how to encourage others to let out theirs. Then we get into the nitty-gritty of creating dynamic scenes and stories, and how to make them come to life. At the end, we'll tie it all together into a powerful package.

That's my promise to you. Now, let me ask for a promise from you. Don't just read this book! I mean it. Do something with it. As you read it you'll gain new insights, but only 1/10 of what you'll gain by experiencing it. That's why I've included games at the the end of each chapter to give you real experiences of what you're learning. They've been adapted so you can do them on your own without a partner. Play those games! You'll gain a much fuller appreciation of what you're reading and you'll be able to start using it immediately to achieve better results in your life.

At the end of the book is an entire scene transcribed with comments. It will allow you to more easily appreciate how all of the concepts in the book work together to create an entire world and storyline out of thin air. You may be surprised by how fascinating it is to take apart communication and discover how it works on such a subtle level.

Realize that this book is packed with information, so don't expect to catch everything your first time through. That's okay. Each time you re-read it, you'll learn something new you missed before. That's because you'll be able to build further understandings on top of the knowledge and skills you've already gained. One of the exciting things about the areas of communication and creativity is there's always more to learn. Just when you think you've got it all figured out, you'll discover something new. Enjoy exploring!

If you enjoy this book, please leave a review on Amazon.com. I'm always open to feedback on how to improve this book to make it more useful for you. If you have comments or suggestions, let me know. I may even give you credit in the next edition. Just email me: chad@seattleimprovclasses.com

10 Ways Improv Can Make Your Life Better!

If you want to improve your life, this may be the most important book you'll ever read. Improv is one of the best tools to increase the quality of your life. You'll be surprised by how quickly you'll become a more effective person because of the skills you gain.

You're about to learn a complete improvisation system: 7 simple steps to guarantee your success. It's proven extremely effective for my students, at Seattle Improv Classes, many of whom were literally terrified of improv. People who never imagined they could think on their feet can now do so with ease - even in front of a room full of strangers.

You'll find most people don't learn improv to become actors, they do it to improve their lives. Before you read the rest of this book, I want to take a moment to share 10 ways improv makes you a happier, healthier, more alive human being.

#1 Ace Your Job Interview.

When I ask people why they decided to take improv classes, I'm surprised by how many say that a job recruiter suggested it. They start doing improv as a way to increase their success on interviews.

It makes sense.

Handling an interview with a prospective employer is one of the most stressful situations most people face. Saying or doing the wrong thing can cost you a job you're excited about. And, for every month you go without a job, it can cost you thousands of dollars. That's a lot of pressure.

Meanwhile, if you do get hired, how you handled the interview process affects what you get paid. Strong interpersonal skills can increase your take home pay substantially. It literally pays to be effective.

It only makes sense to be certain you come across as confident, intelligent, and socially capable. Improv is one of the best ways to train yourself to exude those qualities. Because of that, it's one of the first things many experts recommend to hopeful job candidates.

#2 Meet Your Special Someone.

Many dating experts and coaches are recommending improv to people who want to set their romantic life on fire. The world's only dating coach in a wheelchair, Amin Lakhani (aka, The Dating Coach on Wheels, who you'll meet again later in this book) has taken several of my classes. He repeatedly recommends improv classes to his students because it's one of the best ways to gain the skills of making conversations fun and interesting.

Dating is a high-pressure situation for most people. First, approaching someone you're attracted to is something many people can't do. The next hurdle is getting the conversation going and keeping it interesting. Then, asking for the date. And finally, making the date fun and exciting enough to deserve a second date.

Amin and other dating experts say this is exactly what improv makes easier. After you've learned how to stand up in front of an audience to make up interesting things on the spot... Dating becomes a whole lot comfortable in comparison!

#3 Make More Friends.

In this age of Facebook and a thousand apps, many people are more lonely than ever before. We have more contact superficially with hundreds of people, while we share real, honest connections with very few. How can you meet and connect with new people?

Improv helps you get past the fear of talking to strangers. It allows you to overcome anxiety about saying the wrong things, of sounding dumb, of not knowing what to say. You learn you can trust yourself and the other person to keep the conversation flowing. And, you learn the skills to make it fun and exciting no matter where it leads.

People who are confident, fun and at-ease in social situations can attract new friends to them naturally. Improv brings that out in you because it breaks you out of your comfort zone so you can connect with others more successfully.

#4 Success in Business.

What are the most important skills to business success? People skills!

It's clear that no matter how technically skilled you are in your field, having solid people skills is a must to survive and thrive in today's business world. Everyone: from customer service reps who need to calm an upset customer… to CEOs who need to calm an upset Board of Directors… need stellar communication skills to get the job done.

The skills of improv can help you win in just about any field. Salespeople need to understand how to work with clients in a way that builds trust and positive relationships. Anyone with co-workers has to be able to adapt to a wide range of attitudes, personalities and ideas. If you deal with people, you'll encounter resistance and disagreements sooner or later. You'll need a wide variety of skills and abilities in order to handle them effectively.

Improv allows you the flexibility to deal with a wide range of personalities. You'll learn how to build positive relationships and to make people feel at ease. And, you'll learn how to remain calm and keep things moving no matter what the other person throws in your way.

You'll also gain one of the most valuable business skills out there...

#5 Confident Public Speaking.

Many people are so scared of public speaking they shake at the thought of it. The idea of sharing their ideas with an audience frightens some people to the point of tears. Certainly, many who do it still dread the experience of making presentations.

Improv is the safest, easiest, most fun way to get past that fear. You'll quickly gain tons of experience in front of an audience and gain the skills of connecting with them. Luckily, it doesn't have to be a struggle, because you can laugh and play while you gain this confidence.

Plus, you can cut past the boring speech writing, and learn to interact with an audience in an honest, spontaneous way. You can let go of the false protection of a script or plan. That's because you discover you can trust yourself to come up with interesting things to say, even if you have no idea in advance what you'll talk about.

There's a quiet strength you embody when you know you can confidently do a speech on any subject, at any time, without preparation.

#6 Enjoy More Rewarding Relationships.

A woman once told me that after she took improv classes, her grown kids started calling to talk more often. They had previously only called once every week or so. She had tried nagging them to get them to call more frequently, but it didn't work. After she took improv classes, they called almost daily. They told her it's because she's now more fun and enjoyable to spend time with.

Many people have ineffective communication habits that cost them — they cost them relationships with people they love. The habits in how you communicate can drive people away and leave you feeling empty. On the other hand, better habits can draw people magnetically to you and be extremely rewarding.

As you're developing the skills of improv, you'll find yourself being more supportive of other's ideas. You'll see that the people around you feel more at ease and contribute more freely because it's a safe space to communicate. You'll discover people opening up to you in new ways because you accept their ideas and encourage them. They'll enjoy the feeling you're really listening and paying attention to them. Because of that, you may be surprised by how much more they'll want to enjoy your companionship.

#7 Unleash Your Creativity and Forget Writer's Block.

Many people think they aren't creative. There are authors who get writer's block and can go years without writing. They usually say they're stuck and can't help it. That's not because of an actual disease or something about them as a person. Instead, it's because they've learned to censor their own natural creativity. They've decided it's better to shut it down and censor their thoughts than to express themselves in an honest, open way.

As soon as you start improvising, you begin discovering how to drop those old barriers. You discover that censoring is really an ineffective defense against imaginary fears. Quickly, you'll learn you can let your guard down and show your own natural creativity.

Once you've experienced improv, you realize you never need to have writers block again. That's because you're shifting to the creative "right side of the brain" rather than the critical "left side of the brain." Naturally, I've heard many people say their head literally feels different after one of our classes or coaching calls - it's because that shift is very strong.

You'll notice a feeling of freedom when you realize you can unleash your boundless creativity at will.

#8 Become a Body Language Expert.

You may not be able to read a person's mind after learning to improvise, but people may accuse you of it. You'll focus a lot on body language and really paying attention to the people in your classes. So you'll learn to notice what people are really saying — in a way that can make them think you're reading their mind.

That's because improv is all about how to recreate the complex dynamics of human interaction on stage. In order to do that, you need to understand those dynamics. You'll learn about the hidden aspects of personalities and what people are communicating. You may be amazed by how much you discover has been in front of you the whole time, yet you didn't notice it.

For example, you'll learn about what we call Status and how people fight to maintain a dominant or submissive status in every interaction. You'll learn to be a "status expert," as the grandfather of improv, Keith Johnstone, likes to say. Amazingly, status is something most people never notice or understand, yet it is a key influence in virtually every aspect of your relationships.

#9 Gain Awesome Parenting Skills.

There are 3 ways improv helps turn you into an awesome parent:
1. Children are effortlessly creative. Unfortunately, many people shut off the creative, childlike part of themselves at a certain age. When you turn it back on, it allows you to know how to nurture and encourage that in your children.
2. As a teacher of mine, Jerry Stocking, once said, "You can't give something that you don't have." If you don't have happiness and creativity, you can't give it to your children.

By bringing out your own joy and spontaneity, you'll become an example for your kids to emulate.

3.   Kids are generally more flexible in how they behave than their parents. Such parents often resort to force, threats, and punishment to get a child to behave a certain way. Improv allows you to develop a greater flexibility in how you respond to such situations. What may have been an impossible challenge in the past, can turn into a fun opportunity to utilize the new choices available to you.

For example, one parent with a crying child may resort to threatening them if they don't stop crying. Another parent with an improv background may start telling a story and quickly engage the crying child's interest. Within 15 seconds the kid has stopped crying and is wondering what will happen next in the story. What could have been a terrible crisis becomes a fun storytelling opportunity.

You'll be able to communicate with kids more easily because you'll learn how to really listen and pay attention to them. The more that you understand them and how they see the world, the more you can communicate in a way that builds trust and respect.

#10 Stay Young.

Seniors can benefit from improv, too. Research shows it can improve quality of life and ward off memory loss. Many seniors are turning to improv as a way to overcome old fears and to keep mentally alert. Improv is also an excellent way to enjoy positive social relationships on a regular basis. It's a great environment to connect with new friends and to enjoy laughing and having fun.

And, finally, the last on our list of 10 ways improv makes your life better...

#11 Have Lots of Fun!

Yes, fun! There are few things you can do that will give you more laughter and fun than improv. Some people think that if something is fun, it's not useful. They think work, toil and stress are the only things that lead to growth. That's nonsense! You can enjoy receiving all the benefits I've mentioned and be doubled over with fits of laughter, too. You can say things you've always wanted to say and finally just let go and be a kid again!

Learning Improv For Beginners

Tips, strategies, and ideas to make learning improv easier and faster. Even if you're nervous!

The most important thing that determines your success in improv, or anything else in life, is your approach to learning it. Unfortunately, many people have unrealistic expectations and either give up too early or don't even try. I don't want that to be you. You're reading this because you want to learn, grow, and gain new capabilities. So I want to make sure you take an approach that guarantees your success.

There are numerous reasons people fail when they could have been successful:

1. **They believe in the "Talent Myth" and expect to make progress without effort.** There is nothing in your life you were always good at doing. What were you good at as a baby? Nothing but pooping, peeing and crying! Everything else you had to learn. Even things you later learned fairly quickly developed from previous skills: learning to drive a car was made easier by learning to ride a bike. Plus, it was made easier by all the years you observed other people driving. Importantly, you couldn't do any of it as an infant and neither could anyone else - everyone has to learn it.

2. **They keep moving the yardstick so they can't reach it.** Often, you'll look at how much progress you've made and only decide afterward that you should have made more. (If you scored 10 points, you should have scored 20. If you scored 20, you should have scored 30.) You need to set realistic, measurable goals in advance, so you can appreciate your progress. (And, make sure to celebrate that progress, rather than immediately focusing on the next goal.)

3. **People compare apples to parrots.** You compare yourself to your teacher, another student with years of experience, people you see

on TV -- anyone more skilled than you. Those aren't reasonable comparisons to make. Why are they better? Because of a logical reason: more experience, training, and effort. The only fair comparison is to *you* and how you used to be.

4. **People believe movies that dramatize the idea it's not really hard work that leads to success.** Movies often claim success comes from talent, really believing you can do it, and having special knowledge from a grandmaster. Find Mr. Miyagi and he'll teach you everything you need to know to bring down the Cobra Kai - guys who have been working harder than you for years.

All 4 of these things can prevent you from learning improv and anything else you wish to learn in life. They can stop you in your tracks before you even start. That's why we'll take a better approach. What is a healthy way to approach learning the skills improvisational theater and anything else? Take a look:

1. **You always start off bad at a new skill.** If you're learning spanish and you grew up in an English speaking family, you'll be bad at it at first. That's okay.

2. **You have to start with the basics.** You can't jump ahead and you won't be an expert overnight.

3. **At first what you learn seems awkward and you'll make mistakes.** Then, you'll become more comfortable with it, but still have to focus on it. Eventually, you'll be able to do it without thinking - and, you'll still make mistakes sometimes. Riding a bike and driving a car were awkward at first, too. Feeling awkward just means you're learning something new and useful.

4. **Anything worth learning takes effort.** It took you years to walk and talk with real proficiency. Would you rather have saved the effort and be unable to do them?

5. **You can never be expert enough on the basics.** The basics are everything. If you think you've outgrown the basics, it's your ego talking. You always have more to learn.

6. **Keep a positive expectancy and a pleasant attitude.** Enjoy the process and look forward to gaining the skills you're excited about learning. Look to others as role models of what you'll be able to do in the future. That will help keep you inspired and motivated.

7. **The more you practice learning, the better you get at it.** Remember, learning is a skill in and of itself. Some people go years without really learning anything new, so they are surprised when they finally do start learning a new skill that it's challenging. The

more new things you learn, the more you'll become better at the activity of learning itself.

8. The more time you spend using a skill, the faster you progress. If you never spoke a foreign language that you were studying in books, you'd never become fluent. Ever. Give yourself every opportunity to practice and you'll make much faster progress. The skills in this book can be practiced anytime you're awake. And, the more you practice them, the more quickly you'll progress.

9. The only person worth comparing yourself to is your past self. Comparing yourself to others is useless. So look to others solely for inspiration and motivation. Compare yourself and your abilities to how you were in the past. How much progress have you made since you started? How have you grown since last month?

That's a simple rundown of an approach to guarantee your success in improv. (Plus, anything else worth learning in life.) You'll learn faster, make quicker progress and have more fun when you utilize a healthy approach to learning.

Step 1:
How To Be In The Moment.

Secrets to get out of your head, connect with others, and release your creativity!

One of the first things you absolutely must do to improvise effectively is to be in the moment. If you're not, no cool trick or technique will make up for it. It doesn't matter how many rules you memorize or even how much experience you have. If your mind is elsewhere, how can you possibly respond effectively?

I find the most important thing to accomplish, whether I'm leading a large class or coaching one-on-one, is to get people over their fears, out of their heads, and into the moment. There are numerous ways to do that which are very effective. Viola Spolin is known as the grandmother of improv, and she designed a number of games to get people physically in-sync each other. This helped get them out of their thoughts and made them more attentive and alert. She realized they quickly could forget their fears and insecurities by focusing on the other person.

Just taking a little bit of time at the start of a scene to interact nonverbally can help build a connection with your partner. Notice the word partner. It's not adversary, victim or enemy. It's... partner. Treat them like one. Often, people start a scene without seeming to notice another person exists. If they do even notice the other person, it can seem like they're adversarial - because they are. They'll start a scene by trying to create an argument with their scene partner. This goes back to a few things: incorrectly thinking conflict creates interest, the fear of losing control, and wanting to look good.

Let's establish that conflict is a shoddy way to build interest. Instead, the thing that really interests people is connection. You'll notice that what adds spark to classic old movies - like Casablanca and It Happened One Night - is the connection between the leading actors. Often, without saying a word, there's a palpable intensity. We won't always create that kind of intensity in improv, but you do want that connection and presence.

Because of how important being in the moment and connecting with other people is, I'll give you a number of games at the end of this chapter to help you do that more easily. A good rule of thumb is to take 5 or 10 or 15 seconds at the start of a scene to connect with your scene partner and relax. There's no need to talk and it's okay to just breathe and be there. In fact, it may create curiosity about what will happen next. Often we try to solve a problem with something that causes the problem: we try to avoid silence to prevent us from losing audience interest, and the franticness we create can cause us to lose audience interest. Instead, relax, let go, and connect.

Take a breath... Ahhhhhh:)

The next key to is to listen! Pay close attention to your environment and the people in it. That means more than hearing; it means watching, hearing, feeling, smelling and tasting. It means you're giving your full attention to the other person. The more you're in your head figuring out what the "right" thing to say is, the more you'll miss. The more you plan what to do, the more you miss. The more you judge yourself or others, the more you miss. The more you think about the amazing sex you had last night... the more you miss!

It feels good having someone really attending to you, so be that person. The more you attend to what's going on around you - including what people are saying, and to how they're behaving - the more you can utilize it effectively. Ever talk to a salesman who ignored your protests that you didn't want the incredible under-water crayons they were selling? That's the opposite of what I'm talking about. You know in the movie *Miracle On 34th Street* how the Macy's Santa tells people to the department store up the street, because that store what the person really needs? Yeah, that's what I mean. Listening without bias.

Can you repeat all that back? Good, I thought you could! I'm glad you're listening.

It's vital that you let go of your own ideas. If you have a great idea and you force it into a scene where it doesn't makes sense, it's not a great idea. You can't have a great idea in a vacuum - you only find out if an idea was great after you do it. It's merit is based on the response it gets, and you can't know that in advance. If you sit there holding onto an idea you think is amazing until you can fit it in, two things happen:

1. You stop paying attention because you're waiting for your opportunity to use it. So you don't really listen and then miss what's going on.
2. When you do get it in, it won't fit with the changes that have occurred. So, you'll be disappointed with the results.

When you have an idea you really love is when it's most important to let go of that idea. Holding onto a great idea is a form of defense, because you're actively trying to get a positive response. When you let go of the idea you think will get a great response, you make yourself more vulnerable because you're letting go of the illusion of control and opening yourself to the uncertainty of the moment. Dare to find out what brilliant ideas are hidden behind the one you're holding, because there are always more.

Remember to be fascinated by your scene partner. I know, you want people to be fascinated by your wit, your charm, your class, your intelligence, your quick humor, and your universal Godliness. And that's the thing that gets you stuck in your head. Trying to be interesting makes you the opposite of interesting - it makes you dull, boring, conceited, a sponge on humanity, and the improv equivalent of the 3rd Home Alone movie. Instead, be fascinated by your scene partner. Become irresistibly interested in everything they say and do. The more attention you put out, the more you'll get back. And, remember that the more you pay attention to them, the more you'll notice all sorts of wonderful ideas they are presenting to you.

Taking this a step further, focus on making the other person look good. Don't be selfish! You go onstage and you want to be the center of attention; you want everyone to love you, adore you, and think you're the most amazing person in the world. Stop it! Focus on making your partner look good and emphasizing their talents. Make it a point to show off their bright ideas and creativity. Why? It's only by paying attention to them that you *can* look good. Really! If you're off in your own little world trying to think of what will make you look amazing, you'll ignore what's going on in the real world and look stupid. If you're making all of their ideas seem brilliant, you'll look brilliant yourself. Treat your partner like a genius and there's a good chance people will view you as a genius, too!

In fact, you'll often discover how useful it is to aim for being boring. People constantly try to be interesting and it makes them seem dull. Think of all the times you've observed someone trying to impress others and they do the opposite. There are at least 3 reasons trying to be interesting is a mistake:

1. You edit out anything you think wouldn't be interesting. By doing so you edit out your own creativity and only say what you think is safe. (You block your own ideas.)
2. You try to create interest through conflict and merely become combative. (You block other's ideas.)
3. You get stuck in your head and miss what's going on around you. You become a missing person, so to speak. (You block out reality.)

This also means you'll want to forget being funny. The more you focus on being funny, the more you'll be driven by a need to please others. You'll lose your spontaneity and become nothing more than a mere slave to the whims of laughter. You may notice how a lot of comedians tend to be morose in real life. Laughter is one of those things that tends to be as fickle as love: the more you try to force it, the more it moves away. That's because in an effort to be interesting or get laughter, you start seeking approval and acting artificially. People can sense that and respond by being repulsed.

Counter-intuitively, by focusing on the opposite, you're more likely to get the results you want. By trying to be boring, you'll become more interesting because you'll be more present and spontaneous. You'll accept more ideas, be more alert, and respond more naturally.

Another vital key to being in the present moment is interrupting your habits. Remember how when you learned to drive a car you had to think about it? You had to think about which knobs to turn, which buttons to press, and when to look where. Now, you do it all habitually so it's like breathing and you don't think about it. Just riding a bike, reading, and talking, anything you can now do comfortably, you once had to think through and figure out. Habits are excellent because they allows us as human beings to do incredible things. They're truly an amazing gift.

The problem is we develop so many habits that our entire existence becomes one big habit. We don't have to be in the present because we let our habitual responses take over. Our minds are always thinking about the past or future: what used to be, could have been, and might be.

This is a secret key to opening a lost door to an incredible world of possibilities. The more you can interrupt your habitual patterns in how you behave, the more you'll gain awareness of your surroundings. It also opens your potential to behave in thousands of new ways you hadn't noticed. Just because you always take the same route to work doesn't mean there aren't thousands of other routes you could take. It just means you've stopped noticing the possibilities available to you. Unconscious habits limit us because we create them to try to get safety, and safety is typically dull.

For example: if I want to go from Seattle to San Francisco, I could take a direct flight and that may be the fastest way to get there. If I always do that, I might not notice other possibilities that could be more fulfilling. I could take a train and take longer, but get a more enjoyable experience. I could drive and be able to stop in small, curious towns along the way. I could take a cruise ship and possibly see whales on my journey. I could drive from Seattle over to New York, down to Florida, and back across the USA to San Francisco. On that journey, I could see the Grand Canyon and a thousand other sights along the way. Even if I don't reach my destination, the trip could be worth it because of the people I meet and places I go. I might not even make it to San Francisco and still be more pleased than if I did!

As you read this book, you'll be exposed to dozens of opportunities to break out of your habits and respond in new ways. Because you're learning think and behave differently, you'll get new results you couldn't possibly expect by behaving in the same old routine way. Get very curious about what's coming.

Quick tricks to unlock your creativity.

If you're stuck for ideas, it's usually because you're editing in your mind. Almost always, the ideas are there and you just keep passing over them. A simple technique is to brainstorm 5 or 10 ideas rather than just 1. Just focus on reaching a number of ideas rather than a certain quality of idea. In fact, see how many bad ideas you can come up with so you free the creative part of your mind to think of anything.

Will you always come up with all 5 or 10? Maybe not at first. But, you'll always come up with more than 1. Once you take the pressure off of yourself to come up with the "right idea," your creativity will begin flowing. You'll be surprised by how well it works!

You may have begun to notice that we're playing with the strategies you use to come up with ideas. There are numerous strategies a person may use and none of them is right or wrong, they'll just give you different results. Here are just a few examples from what we've already covered:

- They may search for one great/right/best idea, pass by any that don't seem to meet the criteria, and say negative things about themselves while they do it. "No, that's not good enough. No, that's not right. God, I'm so stupid!"
- They could search for a boring or obvious idea. "That seems dull. I'll try it. Oh, there you go. Not as boring as I thought!"
- They could search for a certain number of ideas, without any qualitative judgement. "I could do this one, and that one and that. I could do this or that. That's 5. Wow! I'm more creative than I thought!"

As you continue reading, you'll discover many more strategies you can use to generate creativity very effectively any time you want.

Here's another powerful strategy that builds on that. Find out how many completely different ways you can respond to one thing. Aim for responses that are in an entirely *different category* and make them seem natural. For example, saying something is a very different response than silence. A slap is a very different response than a hug. You can respond to anything with any behavior as long as you justify it.

I remember doing an exercise and the guy I was partnered with said, "I can't think of how else I can respond to you." I immediately reeled off a list of 5 ways. He said, "That bothers me that I couldn't think of any at all and you've got so many..." Anyone can do it, ya just gotta practice. It's like if you're a public speaker and you get certain tough questions again and again. You have to practice finding useful ways to reply.

Here's a simple list of generic categories of response:
- A question.
- An accusation.
- Run away.
- Cry.
- Get angry.
- Get excited.

Let's use those to respond to something in a scene. Imagine your lover cheats on you. Here's an example of how you could respond with any of the items in that list:
- **A question:** "For how long?"
- **An accusation:** "You've been doing more than that! You've been trying to have me killed"
- **Run away:** "I can't take anymore! Goodbye!"
- **Cry:** "Ohhhh..."

- **Get angry:** "You son of a..." Bam! (You slap them!)
- **Get excited:** "Oh, that's wonderful! I've been so worried that you were, and now I finally know for sure! My mother WAS right about you -- I worried that she'd finally lost her touch. She'll be soooo pleased! Now I feel better about cheating on you!!!"

Notice how we can respond to the same thing in a wide variety of ways. You don't need to think of a clever way of responding, or the "right way." You can pick a category of response and justify it. It's a very effective strategy and fuels your creativity.

You can simplify that by simply utilizing emotions. Notice in the last example how you could respond to the same thing with opposite emotions. We tend to think that situations dictate our feelings, but what elicits anger in one person can make another person excited. Changing emotions creates energy and generates a sense of impact. Most people habitually try to keep the same energy and emotion. They go on stage and are angry, and then they stay angry the whole scene - that's their deal. Others pick sad, scared, bored... whatever. And, worse, some people may not display any emotion because they're trying to remain unaffected. (Who wants to see a movie or play with emotionless characters?)

By expanding your emotional range in response to what's going on around you, it drives people's interest through the roof. And, it helps you keep energy in the scene. You can use virtually any emotion in response to anything. Rather than trying to think of what to say or do, pick an emotion and let that direct how you act. It takes a bit of practice, but is actually much easier and helps to create a special quality.

The key is that you have to justify whatever emotion you choose. For example, let's say you're on a date with your boyfriend and he proposes to you. With which emotions can you respond? Let's see!

- **Fear:** "I think that if we get married our love will die..."
- **Anger:** "I told you, when you proposed I wanted you to do it at the top of the Empire State Building! With a live band playing my favorite song!"
- **Curiosity:** "Hmmm. What should I say to you??? What options do we have? If I say yes, will we live here? Will we move to Europe? Will you stop drinking? What if I say no? Will you give up? Try to win me back? Throw yourself off a mountain? Get back together with your long lost love?"
- **Sadness:** "Oh God! I never thought I'd be proposed to... I thought I'd live to be an old maid... (choking back tears) I

suppose we have a 50% chance of divorce, since love doesn't last like it used to. Oh, I'm cursed with bad luck. Yes, I'll marry you!"

By learning to pick the emotion and then justify it, you create a skill-set that makes you incredibly unpredictable and fascinating, and sets your creativity free. Plus, as you gain practice on stage and in scenes, you'll begin to having a stunning revelation - your response *doesn't* have to dictated by the outside environment. You *don't* have to be a puppet or feel like a ping-pong ball being knocked around by the world. If someone yells at you, you needn't feel hurt, sad, or angry. You can respond with excitement, lust, or curiosity. That can surprise the other person out of their negative mindset and liberate you. What could have turned into a fight will go into a more productive direction. You may even look forward to such things happening, as an opportunity to enjoy your new flexibility.

Games

Here are 3 games you can play which will allow you to develop the skills from this chapter. These are all adapted so you can easily do them without a partner. Naturally, if you get the chance to play them with a partner, do it!

Mirroring

Turn on a video of someone doing a speech. Pick a dynamic speaker who moves around a lot. A southern preacher is always fun! Now, mirror them. Pretend you are an exact mirror and copy them as fully as possible. If they turn their head, you turn yours. If they lift a hand high in the air, you copy that. Match everything: gestures, posture, head movements… everything!

Notice how much attention you have to put out. If you go inside your head, you'll miss something. Also, be aware of what it's like to move differently than you normally do. Try this with a few different people and notice the changes in how you feel because of moving your body in a new way.

Break Habits

There are a wide range of habits available for you to dismantle. Anything you normally do with one hand can be done with the other. Are you right-handed? Try writing with your left hand! Also, try eating with the silverware in your left hand! Now pick up a book and read it… upside down! (You'll probably read more slowly.) Find 10 habits and break 'em!

Notice what happens. Do you have to pay more attention to what you're doing? Do you lose attention and unconsciously put the silverware back in your normal hand? What happens when you're mind tries to wander?

Speak Then Do

Set a timer for 10 minutes and begin. Before you do anything, you have to say what it is first. Want to lift your hand to scratch your cheek? Before you do, you'll say, "I'm going to lift my hand to scratch my cheek." Want to walk to the other side of the room? You'll first say, "I'm going to walk to the other side of the room." Want to walk back? Say it first.

You can break this into as small of chunks as you wish. Walking is actually made up of many movements, so find out how many you can narrate. "I'm going to lift my left foot. I'm going to move it 6 inches forward. I'm going to place it on the ground…"

Notice how this interrupts your habitual think-then-move response. After doing this, you may notice how common it is for you to walk across the room without being aware of the process of walking. You just suddenly get their unconsciously. This simple game will help make you more aware during the trip. Also, remember that each piece of the process is an aspect that can be altered and played with. After all, you don't have to walk. You could run, skip, crawl, walk backwards, or wiggle. You can do it fast, slow, super-slow, smoothly, or jerkily. And, you could even stop short after going part way, without reaching your destination.

Step 2:
The Key to Starting Powerfully.

Guarantee you start off strong... for dating, work and life!

Ever tripped up over what to say? Did you get asked a question on a date or job interview only to feel clumsy and awkward? Do you clam up and get tongue-tied in stressful situations? Do you get writer's block? What about public speaker's block? Imagine you're asked to do a speech last minute. They just grab you, throw you on stage and expect you to talk confidently to a group of people. Can you? How do you even begin? Would you sputter and cough? Would you say, "I'm sorry, I can't!" What would you do?

My goal is that my students can confidently handle exactly that kind of situation. By the end of their first class series with me, I want them to be able to come in front of the group and do an improvised speech on any topic. This chapter contains one of the biggest secrets of making that easy to do. It contains a simple tool to guarantee you sound as smooth, classy, confident, and sophisticated as you are inside. Plus, if you get derailed and can't think of what to say, it will be a lifesaver to rescue you from distress. You may be surprised to find it starts before you say a single word.

Let's take a detour first. Right now I'm sitting and looking at the bookshelf I got today. Do you know how to build a bookshelf? Simple. You take two pieces of wood and put them together. Then, add another piece. Then, add another. Eventually, you've made a bookshelf! What color will the bookshelf be? It depends on what color the wood is you're using to build it. You can't expect dark redwood to suddenly be bright white when it's all put together.

How is that connected to improvisation? It will be obvious in a minute. To start with, let's play an improv game that will begin to demonstrate how this concept works. I'm going to start a sentence and you fill in the blank for me. Got it? Good!

The watermelon is _____.

Did you fill in the blank? Great! You're doing awesome! Let's have another go, fill in this blank:

The weather is _____.

Excellent! Do it a few more times:

I'm feeling _____.

My cousin is a _____.

I once went _____.

I love to _____.

You were able to fill those in, right? Yay! That's all you had to do. Pretty simple, isn't it? Now, read on.

I don't know if you said the watermelon is fresh, ripe, green, tasty or rotten. I also don't know if you said you love to kayak, skydive, read, rest or eat. I don't know any of your answers. But, I know that once you got going, your brain kept going.

"A person in motion stays in motion.

A person tends to continue in the direction they started."

Wayne Newton's Second Law of Improv Dynamics

It's unlikely you said, "I'm feeling table." Or, "I once went mirror." Because that wouldn't make any sense. (If those were your answers, please let me know!) You also probably didn't say, "I love to be stung by bees." (Unless you were trying to be funny, which we covered in the last chapter.) Why? Because you'd already started in the direction of things you love. You'd have to go, "I love to... I don't know. But, I hate to be stung by bees. Heck, I'll say I love to be stung by bees!" And, even without being beside you as you read this, I know you didn't do that! You finished each sentence in the same general direction as it started.

Now that we appreciate this simple law of human physics: how can you apply this to improv scenes, getting jobs, and finding romantic partners? Elementary, my dear Watson! (Did you know Sherlock Holmes never said that? It's true.)

The first words out of your mouth will set the tone for what comes next. Those first words, and how you say them, will influence everything that comes after. It will influence both what you say and what people expect.

If you're in the middle of an improv scene and you want to send the scene in a powerful new direction, you can say, "I've got an important revelation to make..." What do you think is going to happen? After you say it you pause, which to the *audience* is a dramatic pause and to *you* is a pause to figure out what your revelation is. Because you said it, you're mind will begin to come up with useful ideas. You may end up revealing that you're a murderer, a ghost, the devil, or about to die. You could reveal thousands of things. The important aspect is you took charge and bravely said, "I've got an important revelation to make…"

As long as you know some simple phrases that generate interest and good ideas, you'll always be able to get things moving again when you become stuck. Here's a simple list:

- "I'm learned a terrible secret…"
- "I've just discovered a mystery…"
- "Something horrible is about to happen…"
- "I've got an amazing idea…"
- "I've done something disgusting…"
- "I know an embarrassing secret from your past…"
- "We have to stop a disaster from happening…"
- "I have a wonderful surprise for you…"
- "I've done something I regret…"

After you say one of these, you've set the direction you're about to go. The courage comes from being willing to say it even when you don't know what you'll say next. But, you'll soon enjoy surprising yourself with how easily you fill in the sentence fragment with the missing information. For example, "I've learned a terrible secret…" can be finished by saying:

- "My family is cursed!"
- "There is no God!"
- "Cats are taking over the earth!"
- "My husband is actually my long lost father!"
- "I'm dying backwards!" (Yeah, I don't know what that means either. But, we'd find a way to make it work!)
- "I'm on the FBI's most wanted list for a crime I didn't commit!"
- "Jesus is unemployed!"
- "My heart is 3 sizes too small!"
- "My family has been abducted by aliens!"
- "My spouse is having an affair!"

You see, it doesn't matter what you say. What matters is how you carry it off. Many people would just look foolish or apologize if they couldn't think of what to say. That advertises it to the world! Don't do that. Just grab one of those simple sentences and find out where it takes you. There's an element of bluffing involved. That's fine. Bluff!

What happens if you can't think of anything even after you say the initial sentence fragment? First off, that's unlikely. You'll almost always have something come to mind. It's more likely you'll think you didn't because you're editing and what you really mean is that nothing came to mind you thought was good enough. In that case, you have two main options:

1. You can let go of editing yourself and just say whatever comes to mind, even if you think it's lame. Know what will happen? People will admire your courage.

2. If you really can't think of anything you're willing to say, you can pause dramatically and say, "I can't speak of it!" Then, another person can help you by saying something like, "You don't mean you've discovered the orca bodies!" Of course, you must totally agree with them at that point and state that's exactly what you've discovered. (They are saving your ass after all!) This means that you made a blind offer verbally (which we'll cover more, later in the book.)

The essential point is that whatever you start with will determine your direction. Even the first word can make a difference. For example: "Sadly..." "Luckily..." "Bizarrely..." The listener knows after the very first word that they're about to hear something sad, lucky, or bizarre. This saves you from the need to know exactly where you're going because you don't have to know everything that comes next. You can just set the direction and find out where it leads you. It's a much more adventurous and daring way to live.

This is important from the very first moment you're in the spotlight. If you walk up in front of an audience in a timid, scared manner, you'll set the stage for timid and scared. People will form low expectations. If you walk up confidently with good posture and a smile, you'll set the stage for confidence and fun. People will get ready for that. You create a direction for yourself and set expectations for the audience right at the start. The audience forms ideas of what to expect based on their initial impression of you - based on how you move, speak, and act.

Sometimes people will be apologizing to the audience before they even make it to the stage, both physically and verbally. Their own fears are setting them up for failure. Remember that you literally think and feel different based on how your body moves. If your shoulders are slumped and you've got a frown on your face, you'll feel worse and be more constricted in your thinking. If you've got great posture and are breathing fully while smiling, you'll feel better and have a better flow mentally.

It's vitally important that when you go up you exude confidence. Act as if you were 100% certain this would be the best experience of your life and they are lucky to be here for it. Then, make sure anything that comes out of your mouth sets you up for success. We'll go into more detail in the next chapter on how the start of each sentence can set in a productive direction. For now, the starter fragments above will help guarantee you always have something to turn to when you get stuck or want to drive things forward.

One additional aspect of starting powerfully is the timing for when you start. When I ask for volunteers in an improv class, most people are very timid and hold back. They want to wait until others have gone first before they'll think it's safe to go up and try it themselves. I like to knock that habit out of people very quickly. There are numerous reasons: 1. The longer you stay seated, the longer you can build up fear. You just give yourself time to get stuck in your head. 2. Just like in life, if you wait long enough, you may not get a chance. When you jump in immediately, you guarantee you'll get an opportunity to do it. 3. Jumping in early gives an impression of confidence, even if you aren't feeling that way. Even if you make a mistake, people will admire your courage in going first. 4. The more experience you gain, and the faster you gain it, the more you'll learn and the better you'll get. 5. You'll get done first, so you can just sit back and watch everyone else.

All 5 of these reasons play an important role elsewhere in life, too. If your boss asks for volunteers to do a speech or anything else, you'll be noticed if you're the first one to enthusiastically agree to do it. Especially if everyone else holds back and looks intimidated. Over time, this habit will build up your image in their mind as a proactive go-getter. And, while you may not view yourself that way at first, you'll gradually gain enough experience to change your self-image and feel much greater confidence in your abilities.

In fact, let's now take a deeper look at how you can use all of this in business.

Utilizing This for Success in Business and Public Speaking

This same skill is useful in your business and personal life in a multitude of ways. It's especially useful in public speaking, and can easily be utilized in job interviews, regular conversations, business meetings, and even dating.

Improv Manifesto

Let's pretend you're in a business meeting and your boss asks you for suggestions. How do you start off strong? You turn to strong phrases that send you in the right direction. Things like this:

- "Here are the top 3 ways we can increase profits."
- "There are 2 mistakes our company is making again and again that we must fix."
- "Let me share a strategy that could transform our company."

You say these with a strong, confident body language and tone of voice. What's going to happen? If you start off with a strong opening statement of what you want to talk about and project confidence, you'll set the odds in your favor. You'll be likely to continue in that strong, confident direction. And, you'll influence how people view the rest of what you say because now they've got positive expectations.

This is much better than if you start by saying, "Um, well, I don't know if these are very good ideas." That sets negative expectations and becomes a hole you have to try to crawl out of later. It's a very difficult challenge to turn things around after that. After that kind of opening, nobody is likely to pay much attention - even if you present the best ideas in the universe! (People aren't listening to you when they are asleep, and that kind of start is a sure way to put them into a deep coma.) You're better off starting confidently and positively, with things you know people are interested in.

It will take a little practice to have these kinds of starters available to you to use whenever you want, but it's well worth the slight effort. You'll enjoy the confidence that comes from know you can always create a good impression right from the beginning.

"But, wait!" You say to me. "What if I'm not thinking of 3 ways to increase profits?"

Naturally, you want to utilize something that fits the situation. Generally, you'll be talking about a topic you have some useful ideas about. It doesn't matter if you don't have 3 ideas clearly in mind at the start, because you can keep putting one foot in front of the other.

In this example, surely you can think of one way to increase profits. So you talk about that and, as you're presenting your first idea, other ideas will come to mind. Soon, you'll be ready to present great idea #2. Obviously, as you present that second idea, you'll find amazing idea #3 popping into your brain. POOF! You've made it through your presentation with flying colors. At the end, you can simply do a quick recap of what you covered. Then ask for some sort of action, if that's required. And, finally, walk away confidently!

It's like that bookshelf I mentioned earlier: you keep adding pieces until it's complete. You start off with individual pieces that are attractive, so by the end you've you've got a beautiful finished product.

"But, wait!" You say again. "What if I pick the WRONG ideas?"

They don't have to be "perfect," "right," or the "best." They just have to be good. What determines if they're good? A large part of how you're ideas are perceived will be from your presentation of them. If you present them confidently, they are likely to be viewed positively. If you present them in a fearful and nervous way, people are likely to think they must not be good. (Why else would you be nervous about them?)

Your first impression will impact everything that comes afterward. If you confidently say at the start, "This is going to be mind-blowing!" People will view everything you say after that as more impressive, important, and exciting. You're body language, voice tone, and eye contact - the nonverbal aspects of your presentation - will also make a greater impact on how your ideas are accepted than what you say. Any mistakes you make will be viewed in a more positive light if you've created a solid platform for yourself with these simple steps.

The specific numbers in the above examples also helps prevent you from wandering all over the place while you're speaking. After you've established that you've got 3 points you're going to cover, it helps keep you directed. You won't start talking about irrelevant information. You do idea 1, idea 2, and idea 3. Then, you wrap it up. It's a very helpful strategy.

Fortunately, you can utilize this whether your speech is extemporaneous or you're planning it. Either way, you will become more successful in capturing your audience's attention, exuding confidence, and communicating your ideas effectively.

How to Make Conversations and Dating More Fun and Exciting

If you'd like another example of how this works, let's go on a date. Let's imagine we're at a nice Italian restaurant together. We're looking romantically into each other's eyes. I ask you, "What do you do for a living? How'd you get into it?"

You say, "Well, um, nothing exciting. I'm a _____. I guess I just wandered into it the way most people do..."

You are not getting kissed tonight, buster. Hell, we're not even gonna hold hands!

Let's try this again. **Reverse time: whoosh, whoosh, whoosh...**

I ask, "What do you do, sexy? How'd you get into it?"

You reply, "I have a job that has many fascinations for me. I'm a
_____. There are a few things that make it incredibly interesting..." "And, there's a wild story about how I got into it..."

Notice: it sets the stage for an interesting answer. It will help steer you in the direction of fascinating and wild things because that's what you said you're going to talk about. The very first words out of your mouth will direct rest of what you say. If you want to have enjoyable, fun, and exciting conversations, set that direction from the start.

What if you don't like your job? At all.

"The funny thing is, I absolutely hate my job! I'm making daring plans to get away. Let me tell you about what I dream of doing..."

(If you hate your job, you are finding something else to do next? Right?)

But... what if you're job is boring? And, you're planning to stay? And, there's nothing you'd rather do? And, the story of how you got it is boring, too?

First, shame on you! I'm glad you're reading this, let's get you a better life. That's sad... really sad!

Second, if you say, "There's a really wild story about how I got it..." Then, you will almost certainly remember some wild aspects of how you got it and you can emphasize them. It's gonna happen. The word "wild" can go into a lot of directions. Pick one and run with it. The point is the same: start strong and keep going in that direction. Now, stop being a Debby-Downer and just try the ideas rather than finding all the reasons they might not work. Sheesh!

Luckily, you can also utilize this to help set others up for success. If you're asking another person questions about themselves, ask questions that send them in fun and exciting directions. Don't ask, "What do you do? How long have you worked there? Where are you from?" You're usually not really interested anyway and will quickly forget what they say. (Hell, you've probably already forgotten their name!) You can ask virtually the same questions and frame them very differently: "What do you find most challenging about what you do? What's the strangest thing that's happened in the time you've worked there? What's something surprising about where you are from?"

Obviously, there are many interesting directions you can go with just the change of a single word. "What's a fascinating story from when you were traveling?" "What's an embarrassing story from when you were traveling?" "What's an adventurous story from when you were traveling?" "What's a scary story from when you were traveling?" The person is very likely to tell you something much more interesting than if you hadn't set them up for success.

If they have trouble thinking of an answer to your question, that's okay. First, because you've set the expectation that this is going to be a fun and exciting conversation, that's now more likely to happen. If they have trouble answering, you can do one of two things to help them. 1. You can share a story of your own. This will give them time to come up with ideas and your story will likely spark their own memories. 2. You can broaden the scope of what you're asking. You can say, "Well, how about an adventure from a time you weren't traveling?" Altering the question slightly can help them find an answer. Like we discussed in the last chapter, focus on making *them* look good.

As you continue playing with this, you'll be delighted by how much more interesting and playful your conversations become. This one idea can transmit more more fun, excitement, and success to all the areas of your life.

Here are your simple steps to greater success thinking-on-your-feet:

- Speak a powerful statement of direction.
- State it with strong, confident body language.
- Trust your mind and inner resources to continue in the direction you've started.
- Help others by doing the same for them.

The related essential improv concepts are:

- You're mind and body will tend to continue in the direction you've started. If you start with a strong statement and body language, that tends to continue. If you start weak, that tends to continue. (If you hesitate and wait, that also tends to continue. He who hesitates waits and waits and waits...)
- You don't need to think of everything at once. Take it step-by-step and trust that it will come.
- Your voice tone and body language carry even more impact than what you say. There's no "right" or "wrong" thing to

say. You'll be judged largely on first impressions and how you present your ideas.

- The more you jump in and get experience, the more you'll learn and the more confident you'll become.
- Commit 100% to whatever you say or do. Commit fully!

Games

Here are 3 games you can play that will allow you to develop the skills from this chapter. These are all adapted so you can easily do them without a partner. Naturally, if you get the chance to play them with a partner, do it!

Story Starting

Improvise stories… but, super short ones. Take a simple sentence like, "I remember the most embarrassing experience of my life…" Say it with confidence. Then, come up with a short story about what happened. Now, come up with 9 more.

For example:

"I remember the most embarrassing experience of my life… I went out with friends and woke up naked in a Denny's parking lot!"

"I remember the most embarrassing experience of my life… I got caught skinny dipping at a retirement home after breaking into their pool!"

"I remember the most embarrassing experience of my life… I asked a friend how far along she was with her pregnancy. She said she wasn't pregnant!"

You can play with other starters, too. "The saddest experience of my life…" "The angriest…" "The scariest…" Notice how just the first two words entirely change where it goes.

Actions Speak Louder...

Read aloud from a book. Any book you enjoy is great. If you have a theater play in book form, all the better. Now, read it with different voice tones and body language and find out how it changes the impact. Read it confidently. Read it nervously. What happens when you slump your shoulders? What if you breath shallowly? Try an angry tone of voice. Add lots of ums and ahs between the words and a quiet tone so you sound unsure of yourself. Now, speak clearly and with a commanding voice. Play with a sexy tone of voice!

Find out what happens when you record yourself and watch or listen back. What impression does each version make on you? Can you make great stories sound dull? Can you make boring stories interesting?

Speech of the Absurd

Do a short speech on something absurd, but start with a strong opening. The subject could be Mating Habits of Cyborgs, Turkeys in Bowling Alleys, or Enthusiastic Tables. Anything nonsensical. Use a strong starter like so:

"I'm going to discuss 3 little known facts of the Mating habits of cyborgs."

"I'm going to discuss 2 critical dangers of turkeys in bowling alleys."

"I'm going to discuss 4 surprising benefits of Enthusiastic Tables."

Feel free to use those or create your own. Notice how having a specific number gives you a goal and lets you know when you've reached it. That makes it easier to finish. Try it out!

Step 3:
Generating an Unlimited Wealth of Ideas

How to gain friends, communicate effectively in business, and build confidence in your creativity.

This chapter contains one of the most valuable skills you can utilize to improvise effectively on stage and in life. It will help you become impervious to resistance and setbacks. It's the classic improv idea known throughout the world as "Yes, and..." As you explore this concept, it will give you a series of new understandings that will forever change how you view communication.

We'll start with the basic idea as it's commonly taught, and then we'll explore the concepts surrounding it in greater depth. What this "Yes, and…" thing means is that any idea or reality another person brings to the table, you accept. If they think you're a martian, you accept it. If they believe the sky is falling, you accept it. If they think you're eyes are beautiful, you accept it. (And, you DO have beautiful eyes! Has anyone told you lately?)

More than that, you add on to their ideas. If they think you're a martian, you accept and add onto it that they are an earthling you've just kidnapped. If they believe the sky is falling, you add on that it's because God can't keep it up since he's tired. If they think you're eyes are beautiful, you add on that you can use your eyes as a tool to control weak minds. (And, you do, sexy!)

This is the process that's necessary to building a reality together. It's like making a salad: if every time they try to add an ingredient you immediately pull it out, you'll never finish the salad. They throw in some lettuce, you take it out and put in kale. They remove the kale and add tomatoes. You remove the tomatoes and put in carrots. They remove the carrots and put in cucumbers. You'll never eat! Instead, if you each add complementary ingredients to the salad, in no time at all you'll have a healthy meal!

Referring to this as the "Yes, and..." concept can be a misnomer. Because, you can say "Yes, and..." while not really living by the heart of the rule. In other words, this does not mean that your *character* in a scene will always agree and add. If you're in a scene with your lover and they ask to have another person join you in bed, your character may say no. That's fine. Saying, "Yes, and let's invite clowns!" is an odd thing for your character to do. In other words, there's a grey area. (Um, and sex with clowns is not a grey area at all. It's red, yellow and creepy...)

On the other hand, if you're in a scene with someone who claims to be your lover and you say they're not your lover, that is you blocking their idea. But, that doesn't mean they can just get upset with you and say, "You blocked my idea that we're lovers! Creep!" Uh, no. They can accept what you said and tell you, "You will be soon." Or, "Please, take me back!" Or, "Look, if you want that raise, you'll become my lover." Anything that plausibly accepts your rejection of them as your lover and builds on it.

As far as an approach to getting along with people in everyday life, this idea of accepting and building on other's ideas can be fantastically useful. There are many business applications, because corporate America is a place where people block other people's ideas all the time. It leads to antagonism and hurt feelings. When employers and employees learn this simple strategy, it can create a dramatically improved work environment. Everyone feels more at ease when they realize that brainstorming and sharing new ideas is encouraged.

Here's a nonsense example of a business meeting gone bad:

A:"I've got this idea for marketing with publicity stunts!"

B:"We've tried publicity stunts and they always waste time and money."

A:"We'll train dogs to howl our brand name so millions of Americans hear it at noon everyday."

B:"That's the dumbest idea I've ever heard. You're an idiot!"

A:"Sorry. I'll shut up."

Here's that nonsense example gone good:

A:"I've got this idea for marketing with publicity stunts!"

B:"Yes, that's great! And, how are you thinking?"

A:"We'll train dogs to howl our brand name so millions of Americans hear it at noon everyday."

B:"Yes, and we could train certain dogs to grab our items off store shelves and put them in shopper's baskets without people noticing!"

A:"Excellent addition! Thank you for listening, I feel validated as a human being now!"

Yes, that's a silly example. And, if you greet new ideas with acceptance and add to them, you'll quickly find yourself and the people around you feeling more creative and inspired. And, at an acceptable time, you can review the practicalities. You need to brainstorm first and judge later. It's like writing - if you just let the ideas flow and write them down, you can edit them later. But, if you try to edit as you write, it tends to shut down your creativity and silence your inner muse. Treat your muse well and you can create beautiful art!

You've now got the basic idea, and that's as deep as most people go. But, there are so many more possibilities available. To stop there is to lose out on many valuable insights. So, let's go deeper into this to give you an advanced appreciation few people ever gain…

The Only 3 Things Anyone Ever Says

A powerful way to break down communication is into 3 categories. They are:

1. **Offer.** This is any idea, activity or attribute that someone brings to the table.
2. **Block.** This is when you decline the offer.
3. **Accept.** This is when you accept the offer.

There are different ways of combining these that will cause different results. By recognizing which of these 3 you and the people around you are doing, you'll be able to respond more effectively. You can learn to change what you're doing to fit the person and situation. You'll be surprised by how easily you can gain new possibilities in circumstances that used to be challenging.

An *offer* is when someone contributes an idea or perspective. If someone says, "Nice shirt!" That person is offering the idea that your shirt is nice. (And, it is - you're very well dressed today. Very attractive!)

As you develop your abilities, you can divide offers into various categories: interesting, dull, big, little, blind, or anything you like. In the last chapter, on starting powerfully, we were generating *blind interesting offers*. Blind because you didn't know exactly what you were offering, and interesting because… they're interesting! We talked about how you can say something like, "I've got a brilliant idea!" That's an exciting offer, even though you don't know exactly what you're offering. An offer that isn't blind but is interesting might be, "I've had the brilliant idea that we should go to the moon!" In this case, it's clear exactly what's being offered, a trip to the moon. Obviously, a dull offer might be, "Let's have a calm day inside." (Surprisingly, a dull offer can become the start of a fascinating adventure, as we'll cover in the section on storytelling.)

You *block* an offer by denying it. You could block the offer about your shirt being nice by saying, "It's actually not a shirt, it's a sweater. And, it's getting old and ratty." You're blocking the idea that it's a shirt and that it's nice. It might sound silly at first, but we've all had that kind of interaction multiple times in our lives. We just try to compliment someone on their taste and we get corrected.

(If we look at this from a behavioral standpoint, we've been punished for complimenting them. That makes us less likely to compliment them in the future, since giving compliments leads to punishment. That's probably NOT what the person desires but, if they don't realize this effect, they will consistently get fewer and fewer compliments. Because of that, they may think that they don't get compliments from people because people don't appreciate them. In fact, they've trained people to avoid complimenting them. Absurd, but true!)

Even if someone intends to be humble, they are still blocking what the other person offered. "This old thing, I should have thrown it away a long time ago. But, thanks for the thought." Humility or any other positive intent does not change the character of what you're doing. If you block, you block - even if your intent was to be humble, sweet, or helpful. It's still a form of correction to the other person and blocks their contribution.

You can also *accept* what they've offered. If you want to accept the compliment, you could say, "Thanks!" It accepts that what they said is the case, and let's them know that you liked it. Accepting is allowing whatever the other person offers you to be true. Notice that acceptance is actually a form of surrender. Whereas the blocks were an attempt to control things by stopping or redirecting them. When you accept, you surrender and find out where you end up. It's like the difference between building a dam, to try and stop a river flowing, and floating down the river on a raft. (Note: the second option is much easier and more scenic.)

You can begin bringing them together by *accepting* and *adding* your own offer. You could say, "Thanks, I got it on my vacation!" Now, you're accepting what they've offered and you're offering something back. This builds the momentum and energy. You're building on their efforts and taking an active role in the interaction. Your offer may or may not be in the direction the other person was intending, but it keeps the river of ideas flowing. This is the whole point behind the concept of saying "Yes, and..." It's not just using those specific words, it's accepting what they offer you and running with it.

Keep body language and voice tone in mind. I was coaching one of my students on the phone today and I emphasized this to him: it's vitally, vitally important to realize your body language and voice tone communicate more than your words do. You can say "no!" and mean "yes!" And, vice versa. You can say, "I love you!" and mean "I hate you!" That can be powerful if that's the effect you want to create.

If you're unaware of this verbal/nonverbal dynamic, it will cause you perpetual difficulties. It will undercut you because even though you may say, "Yes, that's a great idea, and..." your voice tone can undercut it and the other person will respond to your obvious lack of enthusiasm. The more you become aware of your nonverbal communication, the more you are in charge of the impact you have in the world. That understanding will make you much more effective at utilizing these tools in your life.

If this is your first time being exposed to these ideas, you may want to skip the rest of this chapter and practice the 2nd game at the end of it. That game will give you practice accepting surprising offers and building on them. The rest of the chapter breaks things down in further detail and has a great deal of information You may be better off coming back to it when you have more experience. It could be an overwhelming amount of detail to process at this stage in your development. You can always come back to it when you're ready for more. It's okay to continue reading it now if you wish to, because it is a lot of extremely useful ideas, just accept that you may find it overwhelming at points, until you've had more experience.

7 Key Patterns and The Results You'll Get

As we learned in the last chapter, the start of a sentence directly shapes what comes next. There are easy phrases to use for practicing combinations of accepting, blocking, and offering. Even more than that, anything you say can be boiled down to one of these. The more you practice, the more you'll notice what you and the people around you are really saying. It's quite an adventure! Let's go through the 7 patterns now.

1.   Blocking

The word no is an obvious block, and it's easy to pick out:

A: "Hawaii is lovely this time of year!"

B: "No it's not."

"No" is a way of putting on the breaks and bringing things to a halt. Of course, the breaks in a car are vitally important and without them you'd be in a lot of trouble. But you still need to know when you're putting on the breaks and when you're pushing on the gas. Otherwise, you may wonder why you're not getting anywhere. Or, you may go so fast you skid out of control.

A: "Do you want to go out to dinner tonight, honey?"

B: "No."

A: "Want to stay in?"

B: "No, not really."

A: "What do you want to do?"

B: "I don't have a preference."

After receiving enough blocks and rejections, people will generally just give up and stop trying. Usually, blocking leads to fights, hurt feelings, and negativity. Especially when one person is offering ideas and they are all shot down, but the other person isn't offering any alternatives. It can seem like there's no pleasing them because you're doing all the work and not getting any reward - in fact, you're being punished with a form of rejection. The word no is the end of the story: you're not going on a date, you're not getting the raise, or you're not making the sale. That's it. Game over. The end.

Blocking can appear to be more safe, because then you'll get what you've always gotten. By saying no to a date with someone new who asks you out, you can seem to be in control… because you can stay home and watch reruns on TV. (What's nice about reruns? You know exactly what's going to happen!) If you said yes, you'd have no idea what's going to happen. You'd be entering the realm of the unexpected and unpredictable, where anything is possible.

2. Blocking and Offering

The easiest tip offs to this are the phrases "No, and..." and "No, but..." This is blocking the other person's idea and then moving things forward in a new direction. You'll notice it gives a weird push-pull quality.

A: "Hawaii is lovely this time of year!"

B: "No, but I bet South America is amazing."

It's similar to pure blocking but, since it keeps the momentum going it gives a the other person more to work with. It's like turning off one road and going onto another. It does block the direction the other person was intending to travel, but it doesn't stop them entirely or make them do all the work.

A: "Dinner last night was lovely."

B: "No, and I hated the music."

A: "You looked beautiful!"

B: "No, and it's because I didn't have time to prepare."

A: "That was amazing sex!"

B: "No, but tonight will make up for it..."

You'll notice that when the word no is followed by the word *but* it tends to guide it into another direction similar to what the first person offered. Such as if I ask if you want to go for coffee and you say, "No, I don't like coffee but I enjoy tea." You can see you're still taking it in the direction of getting some kind of drink. One positive idea was replaced with another positive idea. However, if the no is followed by *and,* it tends to go the opposite of the direction originally offered. "No, I don't like coffee and I need to leave." Not only is coffee being rejected, getting a drink is rejected, and even the conversation is about to end. The positive idea is being replaced with a negative idea. That dynamic can be very useful to discover, as we'll go into soon.

3. Blocking and Offering (While Pretending to Accept)

Saying "Yes, but..." is basically just blocking and offering, only attempting to hide it. A wolf in sheep's clothing.

A: "Hawaii is lovely this time of year!"

B: "Yes, but it's full of tourists."

Anytime you hear a *but* after a *yes* it's a sign the person is about to disagree. They're about to give a reason why that's not right.

A: "Dinner last night was lovely."

B: "Yes, but the restaurant was loud."

A: "You looked beautiful!"

B: "Yes, but I didn't feel it."

A: "That was amazing sex!"

B: "Yes, but I don't feel in the mood for more."

You'll notice that silence would often be more pleasant than this. At least than the person could mind-read for the person who's silent!

A: "Dinner last night was lovely."

B: "…" (I bet she loved that filet mignon.)

A: "You looked beautiful!"

B: "…" (I bet she feels overwhelmed by how much I love her.)

A: "That was amazing sex!"

B: "…" (Oh, words can't describe how she feels!!!.)

In other words, if you feel a block coming on… shut up!

4. Refusing to Do Anything Part I

People refuse to take a position when they say things like, "Maybe, perhaps, and I don't know." It's verbal quicksand and a complete block to progress in any direction. It stops momentum without taking responsibility because the person saying it is refusing to take a position.

A: "Hawaii is lovely this time of year!"

B: "Maybe, I don't know."

Blocking at least takes a position. If you block me, I know where you stand and can do something based on that. But, in this case, the person doesn't even go to the effort of taking a position. It's a way to be lazy, or a way to try to stay safe by not putting yourself and your ideas out there.

This comes from the idea that sitting on the sidelines will be safer. What people don't realize is that sitting on the sidelines IS taking a position - a position where you can't score any points! You have to be out on the playing field to score anything. And remember, it's the players on the field who are out there having the most fun and getting the most reward. Think of it: even a player on the losing team in an NFL football game makes 10 times more money than 97.5% of the spectators. Do you want to be a spectator or a player?

A: "Want to go out to dinner tonight?"

B: "I'm not sure."

A: "Dinner last night was lovely, huh?"

B: "I don't know…"

A: "You looked beautiful!"

B: "Maybe…"

A: "That was amazing sex!"

B: "Perhaps…"

In a scene, this can be surprisingly funny to watch! I was teaching a class last night demonstrating this. The student who was making the offers was getting more and more frustrated with doing all the work. The student who was saying maybe was making almost no effort but kept getting huge laughs. It just wasn't fair! It's not something you'd want to do all the time, but used occasionally it creates a unique and hilarious dynamic.

Even if you say *yes*, you're body language may say *maybe*. "Um. Yes? And???" This is why a frequent suggestion in improv is to "Commit fully!" It's because people will do and say things half-assed and even if the ideas are brilliant the delivery makes them fall flat. Just as we talked about in the last chapter, your body language and voice tone can undercut the most incredible ideas. On the flip side, going into it with complete conviction can earn the most humdrum idea a tremendously positive response.

5. Refusing to Do Anything Part II

You also refuse to take a position when you say things like, "Isn't, wasn't, didn't, and won't." These are all negations and are really a pretend offer and fake acceptance:

A: "Hawaii is lovely this time of year!"

B: "Yes, the weather isn't bad, and I wouldn't be upset if I were there right now."

Do they agree? Hard to tell! They're pretending to give an offer but all they've added is what isn't the case. Part of the problem with that is it leaves you with a mental image of what isn't there. Watch what happens as you read the next sentence:

Don't imagine a purple elephant! Don't think of a bright purple smiling elephant!

What do you imagine? You imagine what I told you not to imagine, which is a purple elephant. If I'd said to think of a cheetah, you'd have been much less likely to think of a purple elephant. But, since I brought it up, that's what you imagined. So negations make us imagine what isn't wanted and what's not the case. If we want to accept and add on to statements like this, it's challenging because we're adding to what isn't there.

A: "Want to go out to dinner tonight?"

B: "I'm not against it."
A: "Dinner last night was lovely, huh?"
B: "No complaints."
A: "You looked beautiful!"
B: "Not my worst look."
A: "That was amazing sex!"
B: "Not bad."

You'll notice in this example how person B sounds passive-aggressive. You can't tell whether they are agreeing or not because they are refusing to add anything definite. They are bringing up negatives without committing to a negative position - which muddies the water even more. When they say, "No complaints." do they mean it or are do they have complaints?

Don't pay attention to negations like these. It's *not* something you can notice when you and others are speaking. I *don't* find it very useful...

6. Accepting

Saying "Yes" accepts, without contributing anything new. It's an acceptance and reflection back to the other person of what they've offered:
A: "Hawaii is lovely this time of year!"
B: "Yes, it is!"
A: "I've heard the surfing is amazing."
B: "Yes, me too!"

Often, in "polite conversation" this will be masked by phrases that mean nothing and add nothing. "I've always thought so!" "Who wouldn't agree?" "That's what they say!" (Who is this "they" anyway?)
A: "Hawaii is lovely this time of year!"
B: "Yes, it's beautiful! That's what everyone says! I've always thought so!"

It's a way of masking that nothing is being added. The other person is completely in charge of driving things forward. If they don't, it won't go anywhere, because the person saying *yes!* is just along for the ride.
A: "Want to go out to dinner tonight?"
B: "Absolutely"
A: "Dinner last night was lovely, huh?"
B: "Amazing!"
A: "You looked beautiful!"

B: "Thanks you so much!"

A: "That was amazing sex!"

B: "Oh, yes!"

Depending on how the person saying *yes!* says it, the other person may begin to resent doing all the work. Or, they may love it and get their energy amped-up by all the acceptance and enthusiasm. There's a time and place for this because you may want to let others take the wheel and just ride along with them. It can be an opportunity to let go of control.

It's also useful being on the other side of it, as a game to learn to drive things forward. After all, if you can't create progress when the other person is agreeing to everything you suggest, how will you do it when they aren't? It let's you see what you're really offering and helps you generate better offers. If you're not offering much that's useful, you'll know pretty quickly.

A: "Want to go to the show?"

B: "Yes!"

A: "Let's grab lunch on the way."

B: "Yes! Absolutely!"

A: "Want to steal a car?"

B: "Yes! Great idea!"

A: "I'm stupid, huh?"

B: "Yes!"

A: "Are you out to kill me?"

B: "Yes! I can't wait!"

When the other person is just agreeing with you, you'll get excellent feedback because you'll get a mirror image of exactly what you put out!

7. Accepting and Offering

"Yes, and…" is well known throughout the world as a key phrase in improv. It accepts what's offered and adds to it, building momentum and pushing forward into the unknown and unexpected.

A: "Hawaii is lovely this time of year!"

B: "Yes, and I've heard the world's largest observatory is on a volcano there."

A: "Yes, and they are searching for planets similar to the earth."

B: "Yes, and they've found enough planets to believe it's likely life exists on other planets."

A: "Yes, and the question is still whether intelligent life exist anywhere in the universe!"

It's like you're running a relay race. They run a bit and hand you the baton. Then, you run a bit and hand them the baton. You keep going back and forth until you reach the finish line. Or, you may forget the finish line and head in a new and exciting direction!

A: "Want to go out to dinner tonight?"

B: "Yes, and I'd love to see a movie, too."

A: "Dinner last night was lovely, huh?"

B: "Yes, and I loved the veal!"

A: "You looked beautiful!"

B: "Thanks, and you made me feel even more beautiful!"

A: "That was amazing sex!"

B: "Yes, and come here for more, Tiger!"

In the world of improv, and in life, someone who continuously blocks, who disagrees, who kills momentum, who refuses to add anything... is just not fun to be around. On the other hand, someone who bravely accepts whatever is offered, adds to it, increases the momentum, and lets go of control to embrace the unknown... is going to be way more fun, connect with more people and simply enjoy a better life. And, since you get to be around yourself all the time, it may as well be you!

In order to successfully do all this, you must learn to:

- Let go of control...
- Accept other people's ideas...
- Let go of your own "great ideas" of what should happen...
- Care more about creating an enjoyable interaction and experience than you do about "being right."

Tying it All Together and How to Overcome Negativity

You may be wondering how to bring together all the information you've just learned. It's a lot of new ideas and can seem like too much to incorporate. It is too much if you just read it. You need to go through and practice all of it - the exercises at the end of the chapter can help you do that. Play with the different types of responses, find out what results you get, and notice what the people around you do. You'll quickly discover it's like The Matrix, an underlying code to human communication.

At first, it's useful to start by finding out what happens when you say "Yes, and..." as often as possible. Make it your default response to accept and build on whatever anyone offers. Notice how people begin opening up and contributing more. When you're improvising, on stage and in life, it's likely to lead you into much more fun, success, and fulfillment.

However, you'll gain even more if you practice each type of response to the point that you can intentionally do any of them anytime. Otherwise, you'll be likely to block people's ideas without noticing you're blocking them. (You'll just think you're right and they're wrong.) Also, it's useful to learn to recognize what other people are doing so you can develop effective ways of responding to whatever they throw at you. With practice, you'll quickly gain a great deal of skill you'll find useful everywhere.

Any time you make a rule and decide you must follow that rule, you limit yourself. If somebody tells you, "Only ever agree and add onto other's ideas. All the time. With everyone. No matter what!" it's very limiting. There are times when that's not the best idea. It's like driving a car: you want to be able to use the gas, brakes, and steering wheel. Imagine a car where you couldn't break! I mean, if every woman who did improv had to say *yes and* all the time, word would spread and they'd have no time for improv because they'd be busy having sex. Rather than going out to bars, guys would go to improv classes to get laid!

We'll be exploring the concept of *status* soon and what we've covered here ties in with that, too. If you want to create a character who is higher status than another character, you may want to utilize blocking ideas in order to do that. Accepting and blocking are an easy way to show relationships, because you'll tend to accept the ideas of a person you like and block the ideas of someone you don't. If you're new to improv and all these ideas, you don't need to think about that for now. But, I want to make it clear that there's not one "right way to do it." These are tools and can be used in a wide variety of ways. It all depends on the outcome you're going for.

Another reason to avoid rigid rules is to avoid blaming others. If you decide it's *good* to accept ideas, but *bad* to block ideas, you'll be more likely to blame others if they break the rules you created. Rather than building goodwill, it turns into a reason to find fault with another person and prove you're better than them. It's more useful to realize that anything they give you is an offer - even a block. Just accept and utilize it as effectively as you can. If you find it challenging to accept something, that's great because it's an area for you to learn and grow.

Let's use this as an opportunity to go through the list and explore useful ways to handle each type of response. As I mentioned before, this is more detail than you may be able to take in at once. But, over time you can review it when you're looking for options to challenges you've encountered. These are not the only options, and I encourage you to create more so you have as many tools available to you as possible.

- **Blocking.** If you're dealing with someone who keeps blocking you without adding anything at all, then you can say the opposite of the result you want. You might say, "You'll probably think this is a stupid idea!" They may reply, "No! What is it?"
  You can also ask them a question to draw them into making an offer. If you suggest going out to dinner and they say, "No." You can ask, "Why not? What's a better idea?" They might say, "There are no nice restaurants nearby. We'd better cook here." That gives you something to build onto.
- **Blocking and Offering.** Accept the block and new offer, then enjoy moving into a new direction or creatively guide it in a direction you'd like. You may say, "Let's go to Europe." They say, "No, let's go to South America!" You can reply, "Sure! And while we're there let's see the Andes mountains!"

  Luckily, if you accept enough blocks, people will usually want to reciprocate. So you can eventually add, "And, after South America, let's explore Europe!"
- **Blocking and Offering (while pretending to accept.)** You can accept and build on what's offered, just as you did in the last one. Or, especially if you're in a real life situation, you can reverse what they said and feed it back. You say, "Let's go to South America!" They reply, "Yes, that's a great idea, but I don't like the summer there." You can say, "You don't like the summer there, but you think it's a great idea. And we could go in Spring!" The flip in which part comes first changes the emphasis and allows you to build on it in a positive direction.
- **Refusing to offer anything. Parts I and II.** If they refuse to take a real position, by saying something like, "Maybe." or, "No complaints." you have several options. **1.** You can repeat it back to them as a question. "Maybe?" or "You're not complaining?" This may draw them out into making an offer. "Not maybe. Yes!" or "Well, I do have a couple complaints." **2.** You can ask a question requesting them to take a stand, "If you're not complaining, does that mean you

like it?" They may say, "Well, yeah, I really did." **3.** You can pretend they took a position and run with that, "Excellent! Let's go there again next week!" They'll quickly learn they need to take a stand if they want to have any say in what happens. **4.** You can create a sense of urgency by setting a time-limit. "If you're not sure you're coming, I'm just going to put you on the no list." They may say, "Well, never mind, I promise I'll come!" 5. You can even accept and build on maybe! You can say something like, "I know you don't know what you want to do. But, if you did, what would it be?" They may say, "Well, if I was to choose, I'd want to go to the circus."

- **Accepting.** Enjoy running the show! Since they are accepting everything, take it wherever you want to go. If you want them to contribute, ask them to. You can ask, "What do you want to do?" They may reply, "Let's go mountain biking."

- **Accepting and Offering.** Enjoy building things together and see where it takes you! Also, you can feel free to play with the previous responses, to find out what interesting dynamics result!

Improving Your Life: Becoming Happier

One of the most powerful things you can do to change your life is to apply this understanding to yourself. The degree to which you accept or block offers from others - and yourself - has a tremendous impact on the quality of your life. It determines how you get along with others, what you accomplish in life, and what you can learn. I'll give some examples:

- If you're talking to someone you find attractive, you may think, "Gosh, I should ask them out on a date!" That's the offer you make to yourself. Then, you may block yourself, "No, I'm a loser and they'd never go out with me." That stops progress and nothing happens, so you lose out. Or, you may refuse to block or accept at all by saying, "Maybe, I don't know, I'm scared of rejection. Perhaps later." Notice how it's still really a block to progress because nothing can happen.

Also, you're obviously going into the future mentally and making predictions, so you're no longer in the present moment. You're mentally gone and can't connect with the person you're attracted to.

- You think of asking for a raise, approaching someone new you'd like to meet, or even moving to another country. You might say, "No, I can't!" or, "Maybe someday." Either way, nothing happens. This can happen so fast you forget you in fact *do* have the possibility of doing those things. You're just *choosing* not to do them. Assuming you're not psychic, there's no way you'll know what will happen unless you go for it.
- Your boss asks for volunteers to do a speech, work on a new project, or help with a new coalition. You sit on the sidelines and others volunteer. If your boss makes you volunteer, you have a *no* or *maybe* attitude about it. "Fine! I'll do it, geez." Everyone can tell you don't want to do it or that you at least are resistant.
- Your spouse asks you to take dance lessons with them. You say, "No way! I have two left feet and neither of them is mine!" You miss out on the opportunity to learn something new and to enjoy a pleasurable experience with your spouse. (An experience that tends to lead to sex, by the way...)

All of these are opportunities to push out of your comfort zone and find out what happens. Blocking and finding excuses is a way to avoid risk - and, it puts you more in your head. Just accepting and jumping into opportunities will begin leading you into new experiences and new learnings. Will things always go the way you want? Nope. But, you'll learn, grow, and have much more success than if you passively sat on the sidelines of life.

There can be all sorts of perfectly logical sounding reasons for these blocks. "I'm not that kind of person. I'm not ready. I don't want to. It doesn't make any difference. I can't. I don't know how. I'm not talented enough." There's even this beautiful excuse, "I don't need to change, they do! I can't get what I want until something in the outside world is different." That's fine. You can have any excuses you want and still say yes. Then, you can get curious to what degree your judgements were correct and to what degree they were just excuses.

Isn't it often the case that the outside world changes when we do? Don't we gain the skills we need through action? Aren't we sometimes mistaken in our perceptions of others and ourselves? No? Oh. Okay, I was wrong! I can't believe I made that mistake!

Remember that people will form judgements about you based on this and respond appropriately. They'll make decisions about you as a person. Let's go back through those examples and examine them from the other person's perspective:

- That attractive person assumes you're not into them. Maybe *they* even feel rejected!

- Your boss never thinks to give you a raise, even if they would have. That stranger is gone forever and you'll never get the chance to meet them. You'll never have any clue about the options available to you for moving to another country. All of that because you gave up without even starting. It was all killed as a thought, so nobody even knew about your interest.

- You boss sees your lack of enthusiasm, lack of confidence, and lack of contribution. They pass over giving you additional opportunities.

- You spouse is rejected and stops asking you for dance lessons - and anything at all! Why bother? They may find ways to get what they want on their own. Perhaps they leave you so they can find someone willing to say yes.

You see, saying no or waiting until success seems guaranteed or safe *seems* like the safest thing to do at the time. *In fact,* jumping into the opportunities available to you and learning how to handle anything that comes up *is really* the safest thing to do. There really is a steep price otherwise. And, since the feast of life is short, you don't want miss the opportunity to enjoy the taste of every bite.

Accomplishing Your Goals and Communicating Effectively

Because what we've been covering is the essence of how we think and communicate, it has a tremendous effect on every aspect of our lives. This book would have to be of infinite length to cover them all, so I'm going to cover several that stand out as particularly frequent and influential. If you're curious and inventive, you'll discover many, many more!

Goals, objectives, and asking for what you want.

Many people know exactly what they don't like, don't want, and can't stand (the 5th pattern, Refusing to Do Anything Part II.) Because they spend all their time thinking and talking about what they don't want, that's what they focus on. It leads to incredible negativity:

- "I'm tired of working so hard."
- "I don't like our sex life."
- "I don't like feeling so lonely."

The people thinking these thoughts are focused entirely on the problems in their lives and what they don't like. If asked what they want to move toward, they often won't know. They will be confused by the question because they've never thought about what they *do* want. The change in focus will likely make them feel better because they are moving toward solutions and real offers.

Someone who says, "I'm tired of working so hard." may quit their job or whatever seems to be causing the problem. Doing that may cause other problems, such as not having any money! The person who doesn't like their sex life may decide to have an affair or leave their current relationship. That may mean they wind up with *no sex life* for awhile. The person who feels lonely may complain about being lonely to other people. That will chase away a lot of people, except some who like to complain.

If they turn these from negations into real offers, they become more solution oriented and can find more useful and effective alternatives:

- "I want to feel rested and relaxed while maintaining my current activities and enjoyments. How can I do that? Perhaps I can ask for time off. What if I get better sleep or take up meditation?'

- "I want a more active sex life. What if I asked my spouse if they'd be willing to work on improving it?"
- "I want to meet and connect with new people I like and respect. Where can I meet people like that? How can I improve my abilities to connect with others?"

You'll notice it moves from a focus on negatives and what they don't want, to a focus on what they do want and how many ways to enjoyably achieve that. Luckily, you'll notice the mood changing from one of fear, anger, and resentment, to one of curiosity, wonder, and motivation.

After that change of direction, you can utilize the idea of accepting and agreeing with new ideas to brainstorm solutions. Then, it's just a matter of saying yes and taking action.

This change of attitude also makes you more effective in asking for what you want. If you approach someone with an emphasis on what you don't like, they may not know what you do want. You're leaving it as a hint, which means open to their interpretation. For example:

- "I want you to stop being late!" Do you want them to be 10 minutes early? Not to show up?
- "I'm sick of fighting!" How about a vow of silence?
- "I don't like your attitude!" Would you like them to leave? To be sad? Angry? Fearful?

All of these have an emphasis on what the other person is doing wrong, so it likely will make them feel bad. They may become defensive because it seems like you're attacking them. Even if they want to please you, they have no idea how to do so. When they do something to satisfy your wishes they're likely to fail, because they're guessing.

This is a common issue in parenting. Parents tend to say, "Don't run! Stop that! Don't hit or you'll be put on timeout!" As we discussed earlier, the child is left making an image of what the parent doesn't like and of punishments. Since a child's brain is still forming, they have an even tougher time with negations than adults. It's much better to say, "Walk! Come over here! Be gentle if you want to keep playing!" That way they know what you want them to do and what they'll get if they do it.

Remember, too, kids love attention. If you only give them attention when they misbehave, they'll have to misbehave to get the attention they're after. If you reward them with attention when they behave well, you'll find you get much better results.

Animal trainers and behavioral scientists have known this for decades. An animal can learn tremendously quickly when it's taught what you *do* want it to do and communicate that with rewards. Unfortunately, you'll see many people who don't understand this, saying, "Bad dog! Don't jump on her." The dog usually has no idea what they're being punished for, and if they happen to know, they don't know what to do instead. It's much better to just pick a better behavior you'd like them to do, and reward that behavior when it happens. The reward is vitally important, too. Interestingly, people can be so focused on what they don't want, they don't notice when they get what they do want. And, even worse, they never reward others for doing what they wanted them to do. Animal trainers tend to be excellent parents and spouses because they've learned to reward positive behavior the moment it occurs.

This is an incredibly useful set of distinctions. You may surprise yourself with how many places you discover you can utilize it to improve your life!

How to Have More Rewarding Conversations

If you want to have more fun and rewarding conversations, this chapter contains an incredibly useful set of tools. I'll go through a few examples of the dynamics that can transform awkward small-talk into an enjoyable connection.

A fairly common occurrence is one person trying to get the other to do all the offers. This tends to feel like an interrogation.

A: Where are you from?
B: Detroit.
A: When did you move here?
B: 3 years ago.
A: What do you like to do?
B: I don't know. Hike.
A: Where?
B: Anywhere really. Hey, there's a friend of mine. I've got to go!

Person A is trying to get the B to reveal a lot about themselves, without doing it first. Their questions are very slight, safe, dull, blind offers that are attempts to bait the other person to contribute something real. In this situation, either person can make a shift and create a different dynamic.

A: Where are you from?
B: Detroit.

A: MotorCity! I went through Detroit once and was mugged 3 times. Quite a place! When did you move here?

B: I moved here 3 years ago.

A: Ah, so you're used to all the hipsters and tech geeks out here by now. What do you like to do?

B: Yeah, I've gotten used to the craziness. What do I like to do? Hike.

A: Yeah? The hiking out here is awesome! There's a place called Raptor Ridge where some say the last dinosaurs walk. It could just be all the drugged out hippies who are seeing them though. Where do you like to hike?

B: Anywhere really. I've never seen any dinosaurs but I've seen a lot of bald eagles out here. We didn't have those out in Detroit, that's for sure. Beautiful creatures!

Notice how when person A begins adding more offers themselves, it's easier for the other person to feel comfortable contributing. This allows them to make a connection more freely, because both sides are putting themselves out there. There's an element of vulnerability involved.

Of course, person B can make the changes just as easily.

A: Where are you from?

B: Detroit. I'd wanted to move away ever since I was a kid. In Detroit city schools, it's the principals that steal your lunch money! What about you?

A: I'm from Seattle. When did you move here?

B: 3 years ago my friends and I all said we had to get the hell out. So, we packed up a Winnebago and took a cross country trip with lots of adventures. You ever driven cross country?

A: Yeah, my family went 8,000 miles in three weeks when I was 14. We accidentally left my little sister behind at a gas station and had to drive 12 miles back to get here. What do you like to do?

B: Ha! That was a funny story. I like to hike out in the mountains. Sometimes we go camping or fishing and I find that very relaxing. But, we will just go on day hikes if we are busy. You ever go fishing?

A: No, I hike and never fish. But, I've always wanted to try. Where do you go?

B: Anywhere really. We have a favorite spot that has a beautiful lake of glacial water high in the mountains. On a clear day it's absolutely gorgeous.

This time it was person B who began adding more interesting and useful offers, while also opening the door for person A to make some offers. Eventually, it's a balanced exchange between them. It's only natural that when one person begins changing how they respond, the other will begin opening up more, too.

You'll also notice the shift from strict external facts ("I'm from Detroit.") to more personal offers of perspective and stories from life experience ("I find it relaxing.""One time my family...") This is important because it shifts it from a simple exchange of boring information to a process of each person and sharing their experiences, perspectives, and feelings. People and their feelings are easier to connect to and more interesting than simple facts (otherwise, the Encyclopedia Brittanica would be much more popular than any Harry Potter book.)

Even if someone can't relate to the experience of skydiving, carpentry, or living in Africa, they can relate to the feelings you associate with those experiences. They can relate to the fear and thrill of skydiving, the concentration and problem solving of carpentry, or the humor and wonder of living in Africa. This can help you make something relatable to people who haven't experienced it or normally wouldn't be interested. In other words, it a way to make your offers more useful to the other person. Naturally, you can utilize this in a number of ways.

1. You can talk about your personal perspective, "I know being a CPA sounds boring, but I love the challenge of it and the interesting people you meet."
2. You can share an interesting story, "One time, this guy was being audited and owed $250,000!"
3. If the other person has shared something you can't relate to directly, you can find an emotional connection to your own experience, "I've never been to Cambodia, but I imagine I'd feel lost in such a different culture with no understanding of the language. It reminds me of when I was little and lost my parents at Disneyland!"

As you play with the types of offers you make in conversations, and how you accept and utilize the offers others make, you'll discover you connect more easily with people.

Connecting with Loved Ones

If you want other people to feel heard and accepted, you may *not* want to make many offers. Often, we're so anxious to convey our own ideas that we don't acknowledge the thoughts, feelings, and ideas of the people around us. If we learn to listen clearly, accept what they offer, and mirror it back, they may experience a sense of acceptance they rarely get to enjoy.

Here's an example: I watched a video from the 1960s of the therapist Carl Rogers doing his People Centered Therapy. This was on a famous recording (famous among therapists, anyway) called The Gloria Tapes. I kept cracking up as I was watching them because he was just repeating back what she was saying the entire time. There were only 3 times in the entire 40-minute session when he said anything that wasn't a repetition of what she'd just said.

She said, "I'm worried about what my daughter will think of me and I'm embarrassed by my own behavior. I want you to tell me what to do."

He replied, "So, what I'm getting from you is that you want me to tell you what to do. You're very much concerned about your daughter's approval of you and you aren't comfortable with your own behavior."

She said, "Yes, exactly. And..."

This is called Active Listening in communication circles. The hilarious thing was that she kept *thinking* he was saying offering direction. She was trying to read into what he was saying that he was telling her what to do. Toward the end of the video, they had an emotional moment when he finally accepted what she said *and* added an offer.

She said, "I wish that my own father was as accepting as you. In fact, this may sound silly, but I wish you were my father."

He replied, "That makes sense. You wish you could communicate with your father like this and even wish that I was your father. And, you seem like a good daughter to me."

The comment at the end, "you seem like a good daughter to me" was the addition. It was very well timed and brought tears to her eyes.

Boiling it down: yesses will tend to encourage another person and build trust and rapport. If handled intelligently, the person will experience a level of understanding and acceptance that's very powerful

Career Success and Earning More Money

Naturally, if you want to be successful professionally, all of these ideas come into play. It doesn't matter if you're currently unemployed, at the bottom of the ladder, a salesperson, or the owner of a company. The concepts work essentially the same in each situation. By making frequent, clear offers, and by accepting and building on ideas, you'll create a positive atmosphere that fosters communication and acceptance.

If you're going into job interviews, you'll want to connect with your interviewer. You'll want to be relatable and full of energetic drive. If you block and refuse to make useful offers, they won't see you as a contribution to the work environment and you'll come across as insecure or negative. If you're genuinely positive and know how to guide the interview in a productive direction, they'll look forward to working with you much more enthusiastically.

If you're at the bottom of the corporate ladder, it's useful to be seen as someone who brings solutions to the table. If you say no very often, you'll be viewed as being limited. If you always say yes, contribute ideas, and build on the ideas of others, people will enjoy working with you more and view you as an important asset to the company.

If you're a salesperson, you'll be much more effective when you connect with your clients. Many salespeople are straight-up rude to the people they wish to do business with. If their prospect has any hesitations or concerns about purchasing, many salespeople view them as an enemy to be destroyed. (I once saw a sales manager bring a young bride to tears from sales pressure!) Salespeople want to "overcome the objection," so they get into a fight with the customer. "You're wrong! You'll never get as good of a deal as you can from me!" (Equivalent to the guys who argue with women they are attracted to, "You're wrong! You're boyfriend will never please you like I can!") It's much more useful to accept the other person's perspective as equally valid and get curious about possibilities. "Yes, it's important that you get what you need. And, let's explore and see how that could be possible together." Even if they can't do business with you then, you'll gain more referrals and repeat business by treating people with respect.

If you run a company, you'll need to master these ideas yourself *and* help your employees utilize them. If your business meetings are riddled with people blocking ideas and refusing to make offers, they'll become complete wastes of time and in many ways can cost you money and valuable employees. You can't afford to let negativity and fear flush morale and productivity down the toilet. If you hire intelligent, creative people, you'll want to foster their creativity in every way possible.

A good general rule of thumb in companies is to make sure to delineate between brainstorming opportunities and times for critical analyses. There should be times for people to let ideas flow without fear of criticism. There should be other times to analyse those ideas for weaknesses, to guarantee you only put into action ideas that likely to succeed. These must come at explicitly separate time, otherwise people will try to contribute ideas and will be hurt when weaknesses are instantly pointed out. If someone tries to find fault with ideas while brainstorming, they need to be reminded that analysis happens later. *First*, create a safe playground for ideas and explore them in all directions. *Afterward*, put on your analytical hat to make sure they are sound. You'll get more creativity and generate a happier working environment.

Games

Here are 3 games you can play that will allow you to develop the skills from this chapter. These are all adapted so you can easily do them without a partner. Naturally, if you get the chance to play them with a partner, do it!

Yes, No, Maybe So...

Go ahead and make up a story one sentence at a time. For each new sentence, use one of the 7 kinds of response. Find out how it feels. For example, this would be blocking and adding with "No, but..." and "No, and..."

"Once upon a time I went to a distant village. No, it wasn't distant, but it was beautiful. No, it wasn't beautiful, and it smelled of rotten eggs. No, that's not right, but it smelled of something horrible and I wanted to leave. No, I didn't want to leave, and I loved the people there. No, the people sucked but I enjoyed the music. No, it was ugly and the view made it worse."

You'll notice that's some tough slogging! Now, let's try "yes and..."

"Once upon a time I went to a distant village. Yes, and the village was filled with beautiful people. Yes, and they created art that was hideously ugly. Yes, and I bought some to show my friends when I came home. Yes, and I quickly met dogs that did tricks. Yes, and one of them led me to a cave…"

Phew! Much easier! Accepting and adding makes it 10X smoother, doesn't it?

You'll quickly appreciate how each kind of response has it's own character and results. Just as important, the more you practice, the more you'll become aware of which one you're doing.

Ultimate Apples to Orange Juice

What do you do when life hands you apples? Make orange juice! Duh…

You'll need a set of the game *Apples to Apples* for this. Actually, you just need any game that has cards with random words on them. I love *Apples to Apples*, and it works great with this game. Since creating my Android improv app, I also frequently use it and just press a button. Since it talks, it's like you have a weird, emotionless friend playing along right beside you!

http://seattleimprovclasses.com/app

Go ahead and make up a story. Start anyway you wish. After you've started, pick up a red *Apples to Apples* card or press a button on the app. Whatever it says, immediately incorporate it into your story. You're practicing being able to accept and utilize anything!

Here's an example, with the cards I've picked up in bold: "Once upon a time there was **a full moon.** I stared up at it from a mountain top and realized **poodles** were nearby. I'm scared of poodles. Terrified. Horrified. I remember as a small child a poodle made of **plastic** attacked me. Then it attacked **sharks.** It was a truly vicious creature. It still brings me to tears…"

To make it clear to you how this works, I stopped after "Once upon a time there was…" and picked up **a full moon.** In the next one, I stopped after "…a mountain top and realized…" and picked up **poodles.** The more you can stop anywhere and immediately incorporate what you get, the greater your flexibility. Eventually, you'll realize you can make anything fit with anything else.

Try it! You'll have fun and be surprised by what you create!

Yes, Yes, and Away!

Let's get personal a bit. Think of one of your fears. It can be anything! Public speaking. Meeting people. Starting a business. Asking for a raise. Quitting your job to travel the world. Anything!

Now, create a story about it by "yes, anding..." it out as far as you can. Then, go farther! You can do multiple versions. Create a nightmare version, then another that's a relatively uneventful story, and a third that's awesome.

For example: "If I went on stage and did a speech, I'd get nervous. Yes, and I'd forget what I was saying. Yes, and I'd stand there looking stupid. Yes, and people would laugh at me. Yes, and I'd run away and hide. Yes, and they'd find me in a closet and I'd have to run away again. Yes, and I'd hide on the streets and become a homeless bum. Yes, and I'd wind up hopping trains all over the world. Yes, and I'd see all of Europe as a bum. Yes, and I'd write about my travels in a book. Yes, and when it was published it would be a hit. Yes, and they'd want me to do appearances and the public speaking fear would be a problem again. Yes, and I'd run out of a speech and wind up a traveling bum again. Yes, and I'd do it by boat that time. Yes, and I'd nearly drown and end up in the hospital. Yes, and the book I wrote about that will be another hit. Yes, and..."

People tend to think they know what's going to happen. In fact, we never know what's going to happen. It's only because we keep a relatively tight lid on what we allow ourselves to imagine that we think we know the future. Go further with it and you begin to realize how absurd your mind is. In fact, you may find that what used to frighten you is now a source of amusement! Who knew?

Step 4:
Captivating Storytelling.

How to entrance your audience, keep them on the edge of their seats, and discover hidden secrets of human communication.

One key thing I get across to my students is that improv is really all about telling a story. If you understand how to structure, develop, and build a powerful story, then you can create improvisational magic.

This is a surprise to most people because so much of improv performed today is just a bunch of gags. You see a grown man acting like a turkey, a lady crying like a baby, and two more people crawling around wrestling. Not exactly Shakespeare. The storyline is missing because they've just put together a bunch of silly games to create ridiculous moments and get easy laughs. That's fine and it's fun to watch such silliness. But, there are so many more possibilities open to explore.

One of the goals of the last chapter's concept of accepting and building on offers is to create an environment that naturally produces a storyline. If two people walk on stage attentively and they make offers, accept offers, and build on what's established, a storyline will naturally develop. It can be a beautiful and amazing process.

Everything is a story, the question is what kind. It's a good story or a bad story. It entertains or it bores. It makes a point or is pointless. It has depth or is shallow. It grabs people's attention and keeps them on the edge of their seats… or it doesn't.

Stories can be used in a thousand different situations and the goals are many: to entertain, teach, and connect. There are stories that have been passed down for generations and have shaped people's minds and hearts for thousands of years. Entire cultures are based on a few simple tales and fables. All religions have stories as their framework. All great speakers and leaders use stories to create a powerful impact in the world.

There are a few common elements that we strive for with our storytelling:

- To fascinate our listeners right out of the gate.
- To keep them in suspense, wondering what will happen next.
- To be memorable.
- To create a sense of our common humanity and that we're sharing a piece of ourselves.

You can accomplish all of this while still generating delightful laughter. Rather than desperately trying to be funny at any cost, you can create an engaging storyline and you'll be surprised by how many laughs will follow naturally. Plus, you and your audience will find it more fulfilling because it will create greater depth and authenticity.

The first step to reaching these goals is an appreciation of our tools. A painter needs to choose what types of paints and brushes to use, what size canvas, and so on. Just so, we need to appreciate the tools of storytelling and how to weave a web to captivate our audience.

Easy Ways to Create a Strong Story.

There are a number of ways you can structure a story. Depending on the context you can keep it extremely simple or make it very complicated. When a screenwriter is drafting a movie they will have dozens of key elements they're trying to balance. Think of a movie like *The DaVinci Code* and realize how incredibly complex it is. In contrast, it's unlikely you'll want to create something so intricate while on stage improvising. The same is true while you're telling a story to an audience while public speaking. Instead, you'll want a storytelling framework that's simple, efficient, and powerful.

The most basic way of thinking about a typical story is this:

1. There are characters in some location.
2. They have problems.
3. They fix them.

Just understanding this most basic of story structures can help you avoid common mistakes that irritate an audience. It guarantees you at least have some characters, they're in a setting, they have problems, and there is some resolution. Think about it and you'll realize there are almost no movies or books that don't have all of those elements.

When people try to make up a story, or try to improvise a scene on stage, the problem is usually that one of these elements is missing. They haven't created characters or a setting, yet try to jump into action. Or, they create characters but they never give them interesting problems. Or, the characters get stuck and can't make progress on those problems to bring them to a resolution.

You'll realize there's a certain quality that each element needs in order to interest us. If the characters are flat caricatures of real people, we can't connect with them. If the problems they encounter are dumb and pointless, it's likely to be boring. If they solve their problems with an obviously artificial escape hatch, it's insulting to our intelligence.

What we want is fascinating, dynamic characters. We want them to have surprising and engaging problems. Then, we want them to solve their problems in an interesting way that makes sense with what we've learned about them and the situation.

That's the simplest way of looking at it. Let's explore this in more depth.

The Simplest Method: The Story Arc.

The story arc is the basic structure of what happens in many stories. Each part serves as a starter that helps send the story in a useful direction. (Just like we utilized in Chapter 2: Starting Powerfully.) The Story Arc is this:

"Once upon a time..."
"And, every day..."
"Until one day..."
"And, then..."
"And, then..."
"And, then..."
"Until finally..."
"And, ever since that day..."

Here's an example:

"Once upon a time there was a poor boy who loved his cow. And, every day his family had little food to eat. Until one day his mother made him sell the cow so they could buy more food. And, then he sold the cow for some magic beans. And, then the magic beans turned into a magic beanstalk. And, then he climbed the beanstalk and discovered giants in the sky who tried to kill him for stealing their harp. Until finally, he killed the giants and was hailed as a hero.

And, ever since that day his family has had plenty of money and food. Plus, he got his cow back!"

Or, notice if this is familiar:

"Once upon a time there was a boy kept in a cupboard. And, every day his step family treated him like dirt. Until one day, he found out he was a wizard. And, then he went to wizarding school and learned he was special. And, then a dark wizard tried to kill him. And, then that dark wizard tried to have him killed a whole bunch of other ways. Until finally, he killed the dark wizard in a way that was very fair and really not his fault. And, ever since that day there's been peace for the wizarding world and he married his best-friend's sister."

The Story Arc can be useful, especially to beginners who are worried about what to say or do next. At the start, you know you need to create the setting and characters. Next, you establish their routine. Then you break that routine and add a problem. Next, you let them try various methods of solving it (their attempts to solve it will often backfire and cause more problems - just like in life!) Finally, they solve the problem and there's some kind of resolution. You end with them going back to their old habits or getting into a new routine that's been changed by the events of the story.

This makes it easy to avoid common mistakes. For example, some people are fixers, they will try to fix any problem as soon as it appears: Got a disease? Here's your cure. Are you a murderer? I know karate. Does your spouse want a divorce? It's just a dream, so wake up. By immediately fixing any problems that show up, they avoid danger and kill interest. In most stories, the more a character tries to solve a problem, the worse it gets. That builds the interest in what happens next until the characters finally achieve a breakthrough and resolve it all.

A challenge is that if you make the story arc habitual, you're stories or scenes can become formulaic. Because you know exactly where you're going with the story, the mystery and curiosity disappear. One trick is that you can start in any section of the arc, such as the middle. Another fun way to mix it up is to make up the story starting at the end and working backwards. A fun example of messing with the typical structure is Stephen Sondheim's musical, *Into the woods*. It's starts like most other stories and, in fact, combines several classic fairy tales. But, the end of the story and its resolution is actually the beginning of another story. It dives into what happens after everything is fixed and *happily ever after*.

You may want to examine some movies and books to see how they fit into the story arc. By learning to utilize it as a tool, you can feel more confident in your ability to generate storylines off-the-cuff.

Another way to structure your story is similar to the story arc...

Generating Greater Dynamics: Platform and Tilt

This is basically another, very useful way of looking at the story arc. It puts special focus on the type of problem you add and how that problem changes the relationship between the characters.

The first step is to set up a stable platform: you create the characters and their relationships to each other and build the setting. Then, you add in a revelation or surprise to *tilt* the situation and disrupt the characters. Finally, you find out how they handle it and end with a resolution or acceptance of the new circumstance.

What does all that mean?

Say you've got a man and a woman on a date and they're having a good time at dinner. That's your platform. Everything is fine at the start. Then, they go to leave and a man with a gun tries to rob them. That's a tilt. And, that's just one possibility. There are an endless variety of tilts that could happen with two people having dinner:

- She reveals to him that she's his sister. That changes their relationship from romantic to something completely different.
- He reveals he's going to die in 48 hours.
- She goes to the bathroom and drops an envelope as she's leaving. He picks it up and reads it. It says that she's expected on her home planet in one week. She's an alien.
- He tells her he only went out with her because he felt sorry for her. (A less outrageous tilt.)
- She reveals she's a ghost.
- He begins insulting her repeatedly in a bizarre, nasty way.
- She offers him a night of passion, in exchange for one favor.

There are as many ways to tilt the platform (which then becomes uneven) as there are atoms in the galaxy (there are a lot of atoms.) The tilt can be from the simple and common, to the absurd and mythical.

The most important thing in all this is how the characters respond to the tilt. If she tells him she's a ghost and he responds by saying he already knew that, then it's no longer a tilt. The relationship between them hasn't changed and it's boring. But, if he responds with disbelief, fear, sadness... strong emotions... then, it will captivate us. The power is in the response of the characters. Even a seemingly innocent thing can become a huge tilt because of the emotional response you create.

Even James Bond, cool as a cucumber under all circumstances, must have everything against him enough so that he is *emotionally affected*. (That's the trick of superhero stories: how can you make someone emotionally changed when they are invincible?) Nobody can relate to a character who is always entirely unfazed. We relate to people who react in a way that seems natural given the circumstances.

Notice, too, the importance of creating a platform. Many people when they start a scene are so anxious for something to happen that they try to create drama and problems right off the bat. They're afraid to build the characters and environment that create someplace for the tilt to land. If you take a little time to create a stable platform, your tilt can land in a peaceful, pleasant place. Imagine the difference in impact if you drop a glass and it breaks inside a rock concert versus at a library. At a rock concert, nobody will even notice. At a library, everyone will be surprised. Or, imagine throwing a rock into a stormy sea versus a calm lake. It's only in the calm, peaceful lake that you'll see the ripples.

Here are three simple steps to creating a powerful story:
1. Create a positive platform.
2. Tilt the situation and relationships.
3. Let the characters deal with it and eventually resolve the new situation.

Powerful Character Based Stories

Thinking of stories in the previous ways is very useful for creating compelling stories where a lot happens. What if you want to emphasize the impact of the events in those stories on the lives of the characters? How can you do that? Or, what if you don't want a lot of action? What if you want a story based on relationship dynamics? What if you want a story like many by Anton Chekhov? Stories where absolutely nothing happens, yet it seems profound.

There are ways to do that. The one we're going into now is called status. Another way to describe it is dominant/submissive. Another way is superior/inferior. Basically: who is the boss and who is the servant? Who is better and who is worse? Who is more powerful and who is weaker?

You can get this across very quickly and easily in a few short words. In fact, you can convey it without saying a anything. Watch how simple it is to get this across!

A: "You're so lazy. Get back to work."

B: "Sorry. I didn't mean to get distracted. I appreciate you..."

A: "No excuses. If you're not more attentive, you'll be fired."

B: "Sorry. My bad. I'll get back to..."

A: "Be quiet."

B: "Forgive me..."

It's obvious that A is in the superior, higher status role. That's clear from the very first sentence. This is different from how most beginning improvisation students do it. Generally, beginners want to be equal at the very least. Really, they want to be superior. So, it winds up being a fight for who can be top dog.

A: "You're so lazy. Get back to work."

B: "Don't you talk to me like that!"

A: "No excuses. If you're not more attentive, you'll be fired."

B: "I'd like to see you try!"

A: "Be quiet."

B: "Shut up."

Can you tell how big of a difference that makes? If both people fight for position, it makes it harder for anything to happen and the scene to progress. Just like in life! Have you ever been in an argument where both people had forgotten the original point and just wanted to win? When neither person is willing to lose, it creates a stalemate and there's no progress. This naturally ties back into *accepting and blocking.* If you read through these examples again, you'll see that when a person was trying to be on top they were blocking. The person willing to be underneath accepted the blocks and built on them. That is not always the case in status, but it's useful to notice as a generalization.

You'll discover some obvious qualities in the dialogue that indicates who is in the superior and who is in the inferior position.

- Insults tend to lower the other person, while compliments raise them.
- Demands and orders lower the other person, while begging raises them and lowers you.
- Interrupting the other person tends to lower them, while listening attentively and agreeing can raise them.
- Blame tends to lower the other person while apologizing tends to lower yourself.

- Short sentences tend to be from a higher status position, while longer sentences that peter out tend to be from someone lower in status.
- Advice tends to be given by the superior person to the inferior person.
- Excuses are given from someone low to someone higher.

Let's go back through the first sample of dialogue and make it really clear how this works.

A: "You're so lazy. Get back to work." (An insult, and an order.)

B: "Sorry. I didn't mean to get distracted. I appreciate you..." (Accepts. Adds an apology, an excuse, and a compliment which is interrupted.)

A: "No excuses. If you're not more attentive, you'll be fired." (Interrupts and blocks. Offers a threat.)

B: "Sorry. My bad. I'll get back to..." (Accepts. Adds an apology, a self deprecation, and starts to make a promise which is interrupted.)

A: "Be quiet." (Interrupts and issues an order.)

B: "Forgive me..." (Accepts. Adds an apology that trails off.)

As you start breaking communication down in this way, you'll begin to see underlying patterns you were never aware of before. It's endlessly fascinating and useful. The nonverbals used within this will dramatically influence it, too. The body language can make the status virtually the opposite of what is portrayed by the dialogue alone.

After you gain skill and practice creating a specific status on demand, you'll be amazed by how useful it is. It creates much more interesting characters and stories - they really come to life. Whether you're writing or acting out a scene, you'll have an easier time knowing what to say and do when you know what you're character's status is. As you gain proficiency, you'll begin learning to redefine your status in life, too.

50 Shades of Storay!

This gets us into characterization. Characters can convey status through many verbal and nonverbal methods. Here's a list of ways:
- Financial:
  - Wealthy, poor or middle class.
  - The quality, age and condition of their material possessions: cars or lack of, clothes, home, electronics.
  - The people they're around.

- o Their neighborhood.
- o Where they work and what they do.
- o Their attitudes, habits, manners and education.
- Connections:
  - o Friends or no friends.
  - o Status of the people they know.
  - o How they interact with those people.
  - o How people treat them.
  - o Fame and societal importance.
- Speech:
  - o Gives or takes orders.
  - o Slang.
  - o Diction.
  - o Gives or takes compliments/insults.
  - o Vocabulary.
  - o Interrupts or is interrupted.
- Behavioral cues:
  - o Posture.
  - o Breathing.
  - o Sentence length.
  - o Eye contact.
  - o Movements.

That's a fairly expansive list and can be utilized, accessed, and relied upon as a tool for creating a more concrete idea of characters and their position in society and in relation to each other.

To create a story based on status, you do two things:

1. Create believable characters and define their status in the world and in relationship to each other.
2. Alter their status.

Step 2 isn't 100% necessary. You can create an engaging storyline without character change. But, it can be much more powerful when you create a shift in the character. If, at the start of your story one character is higher status, you can have it reverse by the end so they are lower status.

Even more ways to create powerful character dynamics.

Here's a list of aspects of a character - besides status - that may change in a story:

- Desires.
- Beliefs.

- Personality types (For example: introverted to extroverted.)
- Knowledge.
- Skills and abilities.
- Interests and hobbies.
- Perceptual position. (Seeing things from another person's perspective or from a removed position.)

See to it that, by the end of the storyline, at least one character has changed in one of these ways. It will create a sense of something deep shifting.

These, and the previous Status tip-offs, are also a list of ways to create believable characterization. Pick a couple things to define who you are as a character and those will help drive the scene. Having specific character traits and relationship dynamics makes improvisation 10X easier.

Also, don't be taken in by societal position. Just because someone is wealthy or the boss doesn't mean they are high status. It's often very entertaining to have the person's status the opposite of their external role. For example...

How this is an easy way you can get a laugh.

It's particularly enjoyable when outward status symbols are the opposite of the behavioral status. This is a favorite in many movie and TV shows and can be an easy way to get a laugh.

An example is from The Fresh Prince of Bell-Air. The rich millionaire lawyer who owns the mansion should be higher status than the butler. But, in their scenes together, the butler makes witty insults at the millionaire. The servant is higher status and steals the show.

On the old Jack Benny radio and TV shows, from the 30s, 40s and 50s, Rochester became as famous and loved as Jack Benny. Again, he was a servant who would come on and tell the millionaire host of the TV show what to do, insult him, and sometimes make him do the sweeping. Audiences never get tired of laughing at such things.

Storytelling for Public Speaking, and Effective Communication

The connection between storytelling and communicating effectively - whether you're public speaking or interacting one-on-one - is obvious, but it's impossible to emphasize it enough. Many speakers forget the vital importance of connecting with their audience. You can drone on and on about all sorts of facts and figures, and it won't be as impactful as one powerful story. Any idea you want to get across can be conveyed through storytelling. And, it will be more meaningful and memorable. Now that you are familiar with a few secrets of storytelling, utilize them to add power and dimension to your presentations. If you're sharing a story about your real life, you can just change what you emphasize to make it more powerful. Describing how personally you changed can be more interesting than the events of the story themselves. By showing how your status altered as a result of the experience, people will be more profoundly affected.

Even one-on-one, explore how you can utilize stories to communicate your ideas. For instance, people are usually more receptive to advice given through a story than they are if you tell them what to do directly. I've always been surprised by how even just saying, "Someone once told me…" and sharing a new perspective as a quote from someone else, makes others much more receptive. I'm not telling them what to do, I'm sharing what I heard once.

Also, if someone you care about is having a bad day, it's usually better to avoid telling them to feel better or trying to say everything will be okay - that can make the person more upset! Play with going into a story about something exciting, fun, mysterious, or humorous. That can help to change their emotional state and makes them feel better. If they are disappointed and you want to give them hope, don't say, "Don't worry, things will get better." Tell a story about a time you were disappointed and something positive came out of it.

This works exceedingly well with kids. I've volunteered at a preschool for low-income families for years. When a child starts crying, many people try to comfort them. Or, worse, they scold them. Instead, I'll say something like, "Yeah, it hurts, huh? I remember a time when I was your age and I fell and hurt myself. It was a day when I had an amazing adventure…" I then go into an exciting story that I make up on the spot. Within 45 seconds the child moves from being sad to being curious. They stop crying and get involved with the story. It's very effective.

Aren't adults just big kids? I've found the same strategy works for adults just as powerfully. In fact, one time my girlfriend was upset and I said, "You know, that reminds me of one of the children who was crying after another kid hit him. I told him about this crazy story…" Pretty soon she was smiling and said, "Wow! That was an exciting story!"

Stories are one of the most powerful forms of communication. You're curiosity, interest, and practice in the art of storytelling will be very rewarding in more ways than you can imagine.

Games

Here are 3 games you can play that will allow you to develop the skills from this chapter. These are all adapted so you can easily do them without a partner. Naturally, if you get the chance to play them with a partner, do it!

Story Arc

Create a story using the story arc. Start simple:

- Just say, "Once upon a time…" and fill in who and what it's about.
- Then say, "And, every day…" to describe how it was.
- Next say, "Until one day…" and describe what changed things.
- Then say, "And, then…" and fill in what happened next.
- Then say, "And, then…" and fill in what happened next.
- Then say, "And, then…" and fill in what happened next.
- And say, "Until finally…" give a resolution and fix things.
- At last you can say, "And, ever since that day…" and gives us our ending.

Poof! Simple as that! The important thing is that you do it. It's only through experience that you really learn and improve!

Platform Tilt

Now, create a storyline by creating a stable platform, tilting it, and finding out where it goes. As you go along, you can certainly have fun adding more tilts and twists in the road. Many tilts can be applied to any situation. Have fun with it.

Here are some example tilts:

- Attempt to sell them your spouse.
- Begin turning into a werewolf.
- Convince them to have an affair.
- Cure them of an injury or disease.
- Discover a book is actually about your real life as it's happening.

- Discover a hidden room.
- Reveal you're actually them from the future.

Want an easy way to get loads of fun and interesting tilts at any time? You can use my improv app, **Chad's Improv Matrix!** http://seattleimprovclasses.com/app (Only for Android phones and tablets.)

Status

Create a story with one main character. Decide on that person's status before you start the story. Now, begin to tell the story and demonstrate that person's status through what happens and how they behave. How does the way they walk, talk, and respond to other people demonstrate their status? Do they always do what they're told? Do they always give orders? Do they drive a Mercedes or an old beater Ford pickup?

After your first story, do it again. Do it several times and find different ways to show status. Do a high and low status of different degrees. After you can comfortably make one person's status clear, do a story about two main characters, each with a different status. Then, create a family. Next, have a character who has a different status depending on who they are engaging with. What can you create and discover? I guarantee you'll learn a lot by doing this!

Bonus 4th Game!

Go ahead and act out each of the stories you just created! You get to be all of the characters! Find out what it's like acting out the stories you just made up. How do you translate the words of the story into actions? How do you transform the people, places, and activities of a spoken story into the here-and-now?

Step 5:
Creating the World from Nothing

Unleash your imagination, even when your mind goes blank!

This chapter contains a great deal of ideas that can dramatically influence how you communicate. As you read further, you may be surprised by the ways you discover to utilize what you're learning.

Ask most people to improvise and they ask, "But, what do I say? What do I do?" Those are the wrong questions! Most of us improvise our way through life successfully -- more or less -- by knowing who we are, where we are, and with whom we're interacting. That allows us to handle many situations we've never handled before. By appreciating this simple idea, it can save you from a lot of stress.

Beginning improvisers are likely to start a scene in a nebulous space. So, you're not sure where they are. If they know where they are, it may be a room or a building. They may even get as specific as a kitchen. Experienced improvisers are more likely to start a scene somewhere specific, like in Rosie O'Donnell's kitchen. That gives them a base knowledge of what makes sense in that environment.

Beginners may walk through where a table was established just moments before. Experienced improvisers quickly show where the different imaginary objects in the room are and remember. That way, their surroundings begin to take on a reality that helps them come up with new ideas.

Beginners may start a scene as a random person, and refuse to create their own name and identity. Experienced improvisers quickly establish exactly who they are and their relationships with the others in the scene. Their identity and relationships help them know how to behave.

All that stuff about deciding who you are, where you are, and what you're wanting... Do it! Be specific. If someone asks your name, say one. If they ask where you are from? Tell them. If they want to know what kind of music is your favorite? Just pick a @$#% genre!

Don't be silly and pretend that you can make the wrong choice or that you're trying to keep it a secret. Answer the damn question with a real answer -any answer will do. The more you add concrete information, the more believable you are. The more you have those specifics in mind, the more you'll have to work from when your improvising.

Try painting a blank canvass and it can be overwhelming. When there are so many possibilities, some people get overwhelmed. But, if the canvas already has an ocean on it, that helps you know what to paint next. For example, if there is a mountain on the canvas and no ocean, that dolphin you wanted to paint won't seem right. Don't make dolphins fly. (Unless you're Stevie Wonder and wrote a fantastic song about it!) Create the setting, so you know what will fly. (Oh, play on words!)

The more you establish who you are, your relationships, where you are, and what you're doing -- the more solid your foundation. It makes it easier to build a scene. Once you have some specifics, your imagination can take off and begin to easily express itself. Let's go step-by-step through the process.

Who Are All These People on Stage?

There are three aspects to the Who in a theater scene. The first is who *you* are. The second is who *everyone else* is. Finally, there's what your *relationship* is with each other. Let's explore each of these in some depth.

1st: Creating Your Own Character.

If you know you're a plumber, that directs how you act.

If you know you're at a customer's home to unclog a toilet, you're further directed.

If you know you're in a bad mood, you've got even more direction.

If you know you're in a bad mood but you also want them to tip you, you know an awful lot.

Once you know you're a cranky plumber hoping for some extra cash from someone he doesn't like, it makes improvising easier. (And all of life, really, but that's a story for another day!)

Imagine someone says to you, "Let's go to a baseball game!" How do you respond? How would you respond if you only spoke Chinese? You'd respond in Chinese! How about if you're a former baseball champion who lost the most important game of his career? Perhaps the mere mention of the game would bring you to tears. How about a child who loves baseball? Probably with excitement. How about a football fan who thinks baseball is stupid but wants friendship? Or, a bookworm who thinks sports are stupid but wants to impress a love interest?

Create your character's age, relationships, job, personality, mood, fears, and desires. There are no "right answers." Just decide. Once you do, improvising mostly takes care of itself.

Do you need to know everything about the character? No. Just a couple aspects of your personality can drive a scene powerfully. The old Jack Benny Show was kept on the air for several decades, largely based on one thing: Jack was stingy. 70% of the jokes on the show were about how cheap he was.

An easy way to start is just to decide if your character is high status or low status. Then, let that guide how you behave in the scene. And, you can easily go through the list from the last chapter and pick a couple character traits that represent that status. Those couple traits will influence you in other ways you don't even notice. If you decide to be high status and use strong eye contact and short sentences, it will influence how you stand, move, and what you say. As long as you keep your focus on doing those two things, the others will almost certainly ride along. You can play with combinations of traits and discover what you can create. It can seem magical at times!

2nd: Who They Are.
3rd: Your Relationships.

As far as you're concerned when improvising, the 2nd and 3rd aspects of the Who in a scene typically go together.   You say different things in the bedroom with your lover than you do in the kitchen with your parents, right? I hope so, anyway...

What's your relationship to the other person in the scene? Are they older and wiser than you? Are they like a younger brother? Are they your boss and you'll get in trouble if you disagree with them? Are they your silly uncle you tease all the time? Are they your closest friend who is the only one who ever learned about your affair? Deciding who they are in relation to you helps create a real dynamic that is interesting to watch. Once you know even the basics of your relationship, you have a lot more to work from. There are at least two useful way to accomplish this quickly and easily.

The first is to subtly endow your scene partners with attributes. In real life, you may think one person is stupid. You might think another is rude. You might think another is loving. You don't have to say that to them because it will come across in how you interact with them. (Regardless of the truth of your beliefs. They may be a brilliant scientist, while you've mistakenly heard they're they were an idiot.)

When you're in a scene, go ahead and just decide what attributes you want to give the other players and subtly respond to them in a way that shows that. Keeping in mind that you usually wouldn't be direct about such things in real life. In the real world, you may think someone is stupid, but that doesn't mean you'll be a jerk and say so. If it's your boss, you might even try to seem like you think they are brilliant when you think they are dumb as an ox.

So, before you even start, you can decide who you think is sexy, ugly, smart, mean, rude, happy, fun, loving, etc. Treat them that way. It will add a 3-dimensionality to how you interact that's more interesting and fun to watch!

Another tool you can use is status. We began our exploration of status in the chapter on storytelling. Your character can be high or low status all of the time, with everyone. You may play low status with your spouse, your kids, your friends, your grocer, and even the beggar on the street.

But, you can also play higher or lower status than different specific people. In a family, you may be higher than your daughter and lower than your wife. Or, higher than your wife and lower than your daughter. You could also be higher than both and lower than a your mother. Or, lower than both and higher than your friend, Bob.

This is a useful way to add flexibility and dynamics to what you create. Few people feel lower or higher status than *everybody* else in the world. You may have a few people who you feel superior to, even if just a little. There may be other people whose presence makes you remember all the dumb things you've ever said in your life.

This has little to do with real-world rank and authority. For example: most beginners will play higher status than their kids or employees. But, we've all seen where the roles were reversed. Just yesterday I heard a kid yelling in Trader Joe's, "Dad, go ask her for another cookie for me!" The dad said, "How about you do it?" The child replied, "NO! YOU GO ASK HER!" The dad then followed the 7 year-old kids orders. We all knew who was in charge. Oh yes!

If you want even more levels to play with, you can play with the degrees of imbalance in your relationships. You might be *much lower* than your wife, but *almost even* with your daughter. Naturally, you'd never talk back to your wife or dare to disagree. But, you might with your daughter. Seeing a family like that on stage makes it all come to life. And, it makes it easier for you to respond naturally, without over-thinking it, because you have your status to guide you.

What if another person decided they are higher status than you, and you've decided you're higher status than them? STATUS WARS! It can create a fascinating and very compelling situation. Ideally, one of you will eventually accept losing and become lower status than the other. However, one of you has to be willing to lose. Otherwise, you end up with a long stalemate and it gets boring because it doesn't go anywhere. One of you must be willing to let go and let the other person be above you for there to be a shift. This creates the fascinating changes in character we went over in the chapter on storytelling.

Can you now appreciate how this can impact your life? These are two of the most powerful tools from improv that dramatically change your interactions with other people. Status alone can drastically change how you communicate with others in your life. Rather than fighting for a certain status - which is what most people do - you can dance through different status levels. You'll discover it's all an act, and it's okay to be viewed as any status - high or low - because it's all made up! You can adjust to fit who you're communicating with so they are more comfortable because you're communicating in the way they need.

And, by noticing how you're endowing another person with certain qualities, you can begin to do it consciously. Isn't it possible that someone you typically think is stupid will act smarter if you endow them with intelligence? Couldn't it be the case that people you think are cold and distant behave that way because that's how you feel about them? How will they behave when you treat them like they are warm and kind? Who knows!

(Many, many studies show that the same group of kids will perform dramatically differently based on what the teacher was told at the start of the school year. If the teacher was told the kids were bright, intelligent, and excited, by the end of the year the kids are performing above average. If they are told the kids are dumb, unruly, and incorrigible, the kids act that way. Your expectations make a huge difference!)

Again and again I've found status in particular to be one of the most powerful tools for helping my students improve the quality of their lives. In just a couple classes or coaching calls, I've seen it have a profound impact on how people communicate!

Where am I? Creating a Greenhouse for Ideas.

Imagine walking into an empty room that's completely without distinction. All the walls are the same color. No windows. No chairs. Nothing. You don't even know which way is east and which is west. It's an odd experience. You don't have anything to reference off. Everything is the same. You don't know the purpose of the room. You don't know who uses it. It's eerie.

Now, imagine being in a room you know. You know where everything is. You know who is typically there? You know how it's used? It's a very different experience!

When you're improvising, it helps tremendously to begin imagining what the space is like. What does the space look like? What's it used for? By who?

Why is this important? Because, you'd behave very different in the White House than you would in your dining room at home. You act different in your bedroom at night than you do at a bowling alley. You act different in your bedroom at home than you do in your parents bedroom! (Right? RIGHT?? I hope so…)

By imagining the space around you, you give yourself something to work from. A foundation for creation. More than that, you help create a reality for your audience that makes it easier for them to suspend their disbelief. If you use a table in a scene and then walk through it later, that's weird for the audience. Why did you walk through a table? Do you have magic powers? Oh, it was just because you weren't paying attention and didn't notice you did it? Damn! Or, you're using an object and it keeps changing form. First it's big, then it seems smaller and smaller because of how you handle it. No, wait, it's bigger again! Or, the cup you're drinking from is miraculously full of unlimited amounts of orange juice. You just keep drinking. And, the way you're drinking looks like you should have liquid pouring all over your face.

It's a reason to be attentive. And, it's another exercise in how to become more alert and in the moment. You can measure your awareness by how many invisible tables you don't walk through!

Creating Ideas From Thin Air.

We tend to be control freaks. Does that include you? If you want to let go of control - plus make it look like you're reading another person's mind - here's how!

A *blind offer* is when you make an offer to someone without knowing what it is. You can make physical offers or verbal offers. A *verbal offer* could be virtually anything, such as, "You're an alien." In this case, you're defining exactly what the offer is. A *verbal blind offer* would be something like, "You told me you had a revelation to make. What is it?" You have no idea what the revelation is, but you're setting them up to make it. Since you made an offer and you don't really know what it is - it's a *blind offer*.

A *physical offer* would be handing someone an invisible object and saying, "Here's your luggage!" In that case, you told them what you were giving them. A *physical blind offer* is when you hand an invisible object to someone and don't know what it is. You say, "Here's what you asked for!" They can say, "Oh, you finally brought the shovel/penguin/magic wand/diaper!" Notice, it's through the use of words that the offer becomes defined clearly.

Observe how with a blind offer you're giving up control and finding out what happens. This can be tricky for some people because they'll often have an idea in mind that they latch onto. I've seen people correct the other person because that person was "wrong" about what it was. I remember in a class, one woman handed what looked like a baby to second woman. The second woman took it and said, "Thanks for the kitten!" The woman who gave it to her said, "No! It's a baby monkey!" She couldn't let go of control - even of an imaginary monkey!

A physical blind offer can just be a movement, too. You can make a gesture with your arms that you don't know what it means. Then, they let you know that you're digging a grave, or painting a wall, or whatever they decide it is. You might think you're raking the lawn and find out from them that you're pulling a rope. You never really know until they indicate it to you.

Doing this creates an eerie, mind-reading, supernaturally in-sync quality. It seems to an observer like you're reading each other's minds. If you just tell them what you're handing them, it doesn't have that quality at all. Don't fight the river, flow with it. Give up control and enjoy your partner's imagination so you can find out where it takes you!

If you want to start a scene, it can be fun to start by just making a physical blind offer. Based on what they say you're doing or what they say you gave them, you find out the initial information about who you are, where you are, and what you're doing. Then, you can roll on from there.

I believe it's extremely important to be able to do just that. I remember a woman coming to one of my one-time classes who had been doing improv for 10 years. She'd been doing it professionally, too. I had her go up for a scene with another person and she could not start without a suggestion from the audience. She was literally terrified at the idea of starting without a suggestion. I thought it was absurd that someone doing this professionally and teaching it to others was dependent on getting suggestions.

A months later, I had a similar experience with another "experienced" improviser who had the same problem and she literally said, "But I ALWAYS get suggestions from the audience!" There's the obvious point that doing improv *the same way every time* makes it predictable, takes away the risk, and eliminates the improvisational nature of... improv. (Chad rolls his eyes) Plus, she was blocking me and trying to defend an obvious weakness. Yuck!

I enjoy taking this opportunity to point out that *all* of the other people in *both* classes - most of whom had zero experience - were able to starts scenes without suggestions just fine. They simply followed my instructions and it was easy. No one had foolishly taught them they couldn't do it! Please remember with everything you learn from me and from anybody else, it's a starting point. Once you find one way to do things successfully, get curious what other ways you can go about it. There's always so much to learn. Don't miss an opportunity!

How to Give Yourself Ideas When You Don't Have Any.

Don't know what to say? Not sure what to do? Make a *blind physical offer* to yourself! We examined ways to set yourself up for success, by making *blind verbal offers* to yourself, in chapter II. That was when you'd say something like, "I've discovered something mysterious…" After you set yourself in a direction with a sentence like that, you find out where it leads you. You can do the same type of thing with physical offers.

A blind physical offer is typically what I just described in the last section. It's when you hand an invisible object to someone else and they let you know what you handed them. Or, you start doing something and they indicate what you're doing. It's blind because you don't know what it is until later.

A blind physical offer to yourself is exactly the same, only you do both sides of it - you both make the offer and fill in the unknown part. You can pick up an imaginary object without knowing what it is. Next, notice how you're holding it and what that indicates about its size, shape, weight, and utility. That will give you ideas as to what it might be and you can indicate that through your words and actions.

For example, you may reach to pick something up and discover it's the baseball glove from when you were 7. Or, the baby shoes you bought for the child that was never born. Or, the treasure map your parents left you. Or, a love letter. Or, an insect. Or, a magic wand.

You can also make a gesture or movement and only justify it after the fact. You might begin waving your arm and realize you're waving to a friend across the street. You could then yell, "Hey Joe! How are the kids?" Or, you may realize you're swatting away flies. Or, you can discover your arm has pains shooting through it and you're having a stroke. Or, you're washing a window. Or, you're a Miss America contestant waving to your admirers.

You can even push yourself at the times when you *do* know what you're doing, by letting go of your first idea and taking something else. If you know what you're picking up in advance, then abandon that thought for a new idea that comes to you. If you start to pick up an imaginary object that you're planning to be a shoe, make it *anything else*. You can decide instead that it's a brush, a mouse, or a snowglobe. Anything other than what you already had in mind will push you to be more creative. It's your opportunity to dive into limitless possibilities. Live dangerously!

Blind offers, whether physical or verbal, give you an escape hatch when your mind goes blank. It allows you to utilize greater resources so, rather than getting stuck, you can always move things forward. Rather than panicking, you can make a blind offer to yourself, or someone else, and discover where that leads. You'll be more in the moment, because you'll be curious what happens next - since that's now entirely unpredictable. It's an excellent tool and an exciting way to live.

How to Utilize This For More Impactful Public Speaking.

How does use of space make you into a more powerful public speaker? By allowing you to create a world on the stage for your audience. I'll give you an example...

I read an article by a lawyer with improv training. He was on a case where a woman had died. While he was giving his opening arguments, he indicated a place in the room for her hospital bed - the bed where she died. The rest of the trial, he and his team would walk around where the imaginary bed had been. On the other hand, there were numerous times the opposing counsel walked right through it. Each time they did, several members of the jury would cringe or gasp. The imaginary world and the physical world really do meet and interact in people's minds. It impacts how we think on many levels.

You can use this during any type of public speaking. As you talk, indicate locations for the things you're describing. If you're telling a story with several people in it, put them in different places on stage. If one person in the story is taller than you, look up to them as you repeat what you said to them. The more you do this, the easier it is for your audience to follow your story. They'll be able to more vividly imagine what you're describing in their minds. It's a subtle and powerful way to make your storytelling come to life for your audience.

What the #$#@ are you doing?

The other aspects we've already covered will often play a huge role in determining what you're doing on stage. However, it's great to get creative and play with new activities you've never done or thought of doing.

Here are some ideas: Racquetball, Rappelling, Rock Climbing, Roller Hockey, Roller Skating, Rollerblading, Rowing, Running, Shovel Snow, Sit Ups, Snowshoeing , Golf Lessons, Hopscotch, Horseshoes, House Cleaning, Household Chores, Hula Hoop, Jumping Jacks, Limbo, Make a Snowman, Make Sandcastles, Mini-Golf, Mommy and Me class, Paddle boating, Ping Pong, Plan and Take a Day Trip, Plant a Tree, Plant Flowers, Play Musical Instrument, Pogo Sticks, Pool, Run through Sprinkler, Sailing, Science Experiments, Scuba Diving, Shopping, Shuffleboard, Stretching, Sweep Floor/Garage, Table Tennis, Taiko Drumming, Target Shooting, Theatre Rehearsal, Trampoline, Vegetable

Gardening, Visit a Museum, Walk the dog, Walk the Mall, Wash Clothes, Wash the dishes, Wash the dog, Water the Plants, Weed the garden! Go crazy!

Beyond the initial superficial level what you're physically doing, is what you're trying to accomplish in the scene. This is extremely helpful for driving things forward. After something important has developed, you're generally trying to accomplish something. You're trying to fix a problem, understand a situation, or feel a certain way.

- If you've just learned you're spouse is having an affair, you may be having an argument. You're goal may be to get her to stop the affair. Or, to kill her. Or, to find out who her lover is so you can kill him.
- If you've just learned you have 3 days to live, you may want to do important goals on your bucket list. Or, get in touch with someone you were in love with. Or, reveal a family secret. Or, find a cure to the disease you that's killing.
- If you just became invisible, you may want to go be a peeping tom. Or, rob a bank. Or, listen in on secret meetings. Or, fight crime. Or, make your enemy think she's crazy. Or, become visible.

The idea is you want to drive things forward by utilizing the responses of your character to what's already happened in the scene. Many beginners want their character to instantly fix the problem, but if they succeed the story is over. If the affair ends, or you find out you're going to live, or you become visible, you lose the storyline and have to create a new one. For a good story to develop, you'll want to take it to the next logical step (logical to your character, anyway.) And, rather than eliminating the problem, it's likely the next steps will make the problem bigger and you'll have to handle ever greater challenges. That continues until your character eventually experience a breakthrough and the story has a resolution.

Utilize the desires and goals of your character to drive the story forward. There's no need to succeed in achieving those goals. Just make sure you know what they are so you can move the action of the story forward. It's similar to real-life. If you don't have a clear goal you're moving toward, you're unlikely to move quickly in the direction of achieving it.

Games

Here are 3 games you can play that will allow you to develop the skills from this chapter. These are all adapted so you can easily do them without a partner. Naturally, if you get the chance to play them with a partner, do it!

Brainstorm

Write out 20 lists of who, what, and where. Just create a bunch as fast as you can. Naturally, you can do more than 20 lists, and you can do 20 lists more than once!

For example:

"I'm a plumber named George with my wife of 20 years. We're at the park and flying a kite."

"I'm an alien alone on a new planet. I'm searching for a sign of civilization."

"I'm a ghost with a bunch of other ghosts at a haunted house. We're about to scare a halloween party full of people."

You can be ANYONE, ANYWHERE, doing ANYTHING. So, enjoy your freedom!

If you want more suggestions, there are several thousand on my improv app: http://seattleimprovclasses.com/app (It's only for Android phones and tablets.)

Act It

You know those lists you just created? We're going to use those now. Take the first item on the list and act it out. How can you convey what's there? How would a plumber named George behave at the park with his wife while flying a kite. Perhaps you start by acting like you're flying a kite. Then, maybe you say something to your wife. Next, you may get a call from a client about a plumbing issue. Those are just possibilities. There are thousands more.

Go through each scenario on your list and play with how to convey it through your words and action!

Santa's bag of a thousand gifts.

Sit down and open up an invisible bag. Reach in and pull out a small object. What is it? A snow globe? How nice! It reminds me of that one I had as a child that sang *How Much Is That Doggy In The Window?* Now, pull out something bigger. What is it? Oh, a fish tank! Wow!

Get it? Keep reaching into an invisible bag and grabbing big things, small things, tiny things, soft things, strangely shaped things, anything! Then, only after you pull it out, say what it is based on what it feels and looks like.

You're practicing making blind offers and filling them in. What you're really doing is opening new worlds of creativity for yourself!

Step 6:
Developing Stage Presence

How you can let go of anxiety and develop a commanding stage presence.

Stage presence: what is it and how you can develop yours? There are any number of important skills to develop your presence. You'll discover that all of them are nonverbal. People always worry about what to say, but that's the least impactful element of communication. I pound this into my students: it's what you don't say that carries the weight. We've already covered a bunch of really important pieces. And, now we can tie them together and add in some special skills that make a huge difference.

In the first chapter, we developed your ability to relax and be in the moment. As you let go of trying to be funny, interesting, or good, you can be in the moment and find out what happens. Very obviously, the more you're in the moment, the greater your presence. And, the more you're somewhere else mentally, the less you'll convey a sense of presence. How much presence does someone asleep or in a coma exude? None. That's because they aren't really there. You need to actually be there, both mentally and physically, to have a commanding presence.

In chapter two, we worked on starting strong. If you start weak, anything that comes after will seem weaker. If you start with power, anything afterwards will seem more powerful. This on the first words out of your mouth, plus your body language and voice tone while you say them. This initial impression will continue to be a powerful influence the entire time.

In chapter three, we developed your ability to confidently accept and build on ideas. It's important because if you look thrown off by unexpected developments, if you try to fight against ideas, or if you prevent anything from happening, you will convey weakness and insecurity. You'll seem scared and like your trying to protect yourself.

On the other hand, if you flow with what happens, build on ideas and roll with anything, you'll convey a confidence. You'll demonstrate that you can handle anything that's thrown your way.

In chapters four and five, we covered storytelling, character, and creating an imaginary world. The more you can take on a new persona, the more dynamic you seem. The more you can create a compelling storyline, the more you have people's attention and the more you have a vehicle for conveying powerful emotions. The more you create the world around you, the more you'll seem to control and command your surroundings. And, the more you're at ease creating an entire world out of thin air, the more you project an aura of mastery.

Now that you're utilizing all of those skills, you can add in some additional secrets to really own the stage.

Shut up! Silence Creates Power.

Do you talk too much? If you're improvising, it's likely that you do. Ever notice the talking head syndrome? That's where a scene starts and each person's mouth is the only thing moving. "Blah, blah, blah!" "Blah, blah, blah!" "Blah, blah, blah!!!!!" Stop it! Talking is often a defense. It's an expression of a fear of silence, a fear of looking stupid, and a fear of the unknown. The cure is to slow down, both inside and out. Look, listen, and get curious. Let yourself settle and be in the moment. Shhh.

The fewer words you use, the greater the impact of each one. The more words you say, the less any of them matter. Talk enough and that's all people will remember about you. Also, the more you talk, the less you think. It's okay to pause. It's even okay to pause a long time - it builds suspense. Just be with your scene partner, your audience, and yourself. Shhhh!

Breathing is key. Many people hold their breath when they are nervous. If you notice you've stopped breathing, or you're breathing shallowly, take a few deep breaths. Just observe around you and feel your body. Feel free to take 10 seconds at the start to just breathe. Shhhhh!

The Way You Move Says More Than Mere Words.

How you move says volumes about you before you say a word! You walk, gesture, sit, and stand in a way particular to you. Just look at your walk. How quickly or slowly do you walk? What parts of your body swing and move as you walk? Where is your body bound up and immobile? Where do you look and focus as you walk? You can play with and alter all of these things and become a totally different person.

If you normally walk fast, try moving slowly. If you normally walk in a relaxed loose way, try being tight and bound. If you normally swing your arms, try keeping them more still. These will create different impressions on the audience and make you look more interesting in scenes. It will actually change what you say and how you respond to others because your body affects how you think. If you're tight and bound up, you'll say something totally different than if your body is loose and relaxed.

Realize part of being an amazing improviser is becoming a body language expert. How much do you blink? How many gestures do you make? Are they fast or slow gestures? Do you speak more to one person than another? How quickly do you reply when asked a question? Do you respond instantly or do you take several seconds to think? Do you laugh a lot? Are you quiet or do you talk a lot? Do you smile much? Do you have straight posture or do you slouch? Do you pace the floor or stand still? All of these things, and many more, can create huge differences in the impression you make.

Plus, if you change one of these things, you're likely to change several. Change your posture and you're likely to change your eye contact and speed of movement. Change how much you blink and you may move around more. Pick one specific piece of body language and focus on that. Find out what else changes when you do that and discover how the impression you make changes. Small things can carry a big impact!

Many people are bound up physically and just stand there. They might be sluggish or tense. Use your body! Move! Make physical offers. Touch. Get on the floor. Move around the room. Crawl. Sit. Stand. Roll over. Play dead! Whatever, anything but standing around blabbing! Just moving more creates an astoundingly different dynamic.

How we move is, in many ways, who we are -- try changing it!

The Impact of Touch: "Let's get physical! Physical!"

It's not unusual to see improvisers look like they're scared the other person has a disease they might catch. They won't go near them. That's not natural! In real life people touch each other. Not necessarily a lot nowadays. But, generally the longer and closer the relationship, the more they'll touch. That means, if you're in a scene with someone who is supposed to be your spouse and you won't come within 5 feet of them, it looks weird! (Unless it's because of a fight last night or that you've discovered an affair.)

Touch also helps slow you down. A lot of people get into their heads and literally "out of touch" with their surroundings. By intentionally focusing on touch, feel, and physical connection, you can become more grounded and centered. One of the games at the end of this chapter will help you learn how to utilize this more easily.

You Are More Powerful When You're Powerfully Influenced.

Have you ever heard this about great actors? "Bad actors act when they're speaking. Great actors act when they're listening!" It's true in many ways!

Many people who try to improvise go out of their way not to seem like they're not influenced by the other person. They argue, fight, block ideas, and do anything they can to seem unfazed. The problem is that the audience wants to see you... fazed! They want to see you surprised, overwhelmed, angry, happy, sad, lost, excited, and disturbed. They want to see you react to what happens, that's the most fascinating part.

Let yourself respond honestly. If your spouse told you they were leaving you, would you make a joke of it? Probably not. If you were threatened with a knife, would you make wisecracks? Nope. So, why do that in improv? (Because we want to be funny. So, we try to make the same jokes everyone else tries to make.)

People can't relate to that. We can relate to someone who flies off the handle when their spouse announces a divorce. Or, who is emotionally overwhelmed. Or even is relieved to finally be free of a bad relationship. We can relate to fear at the threat of a knife. And, we can relate to courage in defending yourself. Or, sadness that you haven't accomplished what you could have with your life.

If you have a bizarre response, you'll have to justify it somehow. It's possible you could make us buy your wisecrack if you're an Indiana Jones type character who, when confronted with a sword, just makes a joke and shoots the guy. But, typically, it's just an attempt to get approval from your audience by making them laugh and will backfire on you. (Isn't that what you get for shooting a poor fool with a sword? The gun backfires on you! Hahaha!)

And, you can show your response very powerfully without saying a word because you can convey any emotion silently. You can steal the show from people who talk nonstop with how you listen. When you respond fully, honestly, and are strongly affected by what happens, we'll admire you for it and be captivated.

A Subconscious Method to Become More Animated.

In real life people frequently go, "Ah! Oh! Hmmm. Ooops! Argh! Ohhhh! Ummm hmmm! Rawr!"

We make all kinds of noises without noticing it. It's a subtle, other-than-conscious means of expression and communication. But, once we go on stage and get nervous, we go into talking-head mode. We don't make our normal expressive noises. There's something weird going on and people pick up on it without knowing what it is.

So, play with adding emotional noises to your scenes and find out what happens. Even if it feels unnatural at first. You don't need to be obvious about it, yet, you'll discover it actually changes how you behave. You'll become more expressive in other ways, both physically and verbally. You'll discover that you come across as more natural and real to your audience. And, if in life people tend to find you unexpressive, this is a way to change that.

It's also therapeutic to let out a good old-fashioned jungle growl. RAAWWWWWRRR!!!!

Getting External Feedback

What's the most effective way to see your strengths and weaknesses so you can learn how to improve? By recording yourself and watching it back. Public speakers consider this a must and it is for you, too. If you want other people to watch you, the least you can do is watch yourself. It's one of the best ways to improve your performance at anything!

Don't like watching yourself on video? Get over it! If you really have a hard time watching recordings of yourself, because you judge yourself harshly, play with judging to the extreme. Remember, you can always accept a negative offer, such as a harsh judgment, and build it to a point of absurdity. Build up your judgments to the point they seem nonsensical, so you realize they are absurd. Then, go the opposite direction and judge yourself absurdly positively. It helps you discover who's making up the judgments - which happens to be you - and they stop seeming real. It's a way you can begin to lighten up and have fun. In addition, after you've watched yourself on video enough, you'll notice you've gradually lost the habit of judging harshly and can just learn from what you observe.

The more you watch and listen to recordings of yourself, the more you'll catch. You'll discover all sorts of things you can do to convey a stronger, more powerful, and memorable stage presence!

Games

Here are 3 games you can play that will allow you to develop the skills from this chapter. These are all adapted so you can easily do them without a partner. Though, the first game uses many unwitting partners. Naturally, if you get the chance to play all of them with a witting partner, do it!

Touch and Talk

Play this throughout your day. Only speak if you're touching someone. Obviously, don't do anything that will get you fired or in jail - be appropriate and intelligent. But, if you want to say something to your friend and they are on the other side of the room, you can walk over there and put your hand on their shoulder before you speak. You can grab your significant other's hand or put your arm around them before you say something.

If you're not touching someone, use grunts, gestures and expressions to communicate. Find out if you can be subtle enough that nobody notices. Discover if people treat you differently without even consciously knowing anything is different. How does this interrupt your normal patterns of communicating?

The Leg Bone's Connected to the...

Play with different ways of moving. Try walking stiffly. Then, try walking relaxed. Play with having tension in your chest as you walk. Now, tension in your buttocks. Then, breathe shallowly. Now, breathe deeply. Keep one hand clenched in a fist as you walk. Tighten your jaw and discover how that affects the rest of you. What do you notice?

Jungle Roar

Play with being different animals. Make their noises and move like them. What sound does a cow make? A jaguar? A bear? How do you feel as you move and make noises like them? Play with it and have fun!

Now, make emotional noises. Make the sounds of exhaustion, excitement, arousal, sadness, pain, love, and fear. Let it out, baby!

If you're having trouble thinking of emotions, there's a button on my app to suggest them http://seattleimprovclasses.com/app (For android phones and tablets only.)

Step 7:
The Last Key to Success

Take risks, overcome obstacles and let go of your fears.

In every class I ever teach and every coaching I ever do, I emphasize this right from the start because it's very important to me. The thing that stops most people from achieving their dreams in life isn't talent. It's not luck or ability. It's not intelligence or education. What stops people is fear. It can be fear of failure... of the unknown... of looking foolish... of making mistakes... of what people will think of you... of people in general. Fear.

I know this because I've always included coaching calls with my classes. I coach all my students on the phone each week between each class. People can be incredibly honest with me on the phone and say things they don't in a class full of people. They'll say things like:

"I want to make new friends because I don't really have any, but I'm uncomfortable with people." "I want to find a girlfriend, but I feel like I'm too shy and boring." "I want to do public speaking at work, but it terrifies me." "I want to connect with my grown children, but it seems like we can't." "I want to write a book, but I'm scared of criticism."

Often people will tell me the same types of things in email, before we've even met. They're open about it because I take the time and effort to ask. That's why I've always focused my classes very directly on how to apply what we're working on to your real life. Because, that's what people want. They don't care about becoming actors. They want to live life fully. They want to be able to go after their dreams and have the skills to accomplish them.

If you let fear stop you from anything, you begin developing a habit of living a life that's less than you want. You can make excuses from morning to night but, if you run from what you fear, you lose. No matter what excuses you make to cover it up, you lose. People will make up excuses to try to put the cause of their behavior on the outside:

"She wouldn't have liked me anyway." "They weren't interested." "I'm not talented, brave, smart, attractive, or rich enough." It takes the direction of your life out of your hands. It's claiming that the road steers the car, while you're in the driver's seat turning the wheel.

There are loads of incredibly powerful ideas, tools, and strategies within this book. You can utilize them on stage to have fun and entertain. And, you can use them to open doors in your life you never dreamed of. What if you didn't have to let fear of mistakes or any of that garbage limit you? What will you have accomplished when you've used what you've learned to unleash your creative resources? Who can you invite into your life with the tools of personal dynamics outlined in this book?

It does require taking action though. What you've read is just words on a page until you use it. It's little good to you if you just read and forget it. But, if you practice each game from the end of each chapter, you'll gain new skills you can utilize. I've given you a bit of a safety net, so you can get started in an easy, risk free way by just practicing at home. Then, you can start expanding to doing it with other people. You can take a classes, and you can invite people over to play. This can be the beginning of a new and valuable hobby. A hobby that allows you to become a stronger, happier, and more effective person.

You'll find your learnings from this book will help you tremendously to get more from any improv classes you take, too. In my experience, many improv teachers put little time, effort, and thought into how they structure their classes. It's often just a compilation of a bunch of games randomly put together with no rhyme or reason. After 8 weeks, people still can't do a scene from scratch. And, there's no explanation of how to use what you're learning in your life. Often, because the teacher doesn't know since they themselves don't apply it to their life. Which, I think, is a loss.

However, you can use what you've learned here to get more out of any class. You can go, "Oh, this is what he was telling me in chapter 3!" If you're doing simple games in a class that might otherwise not be challenging to you, you can also utilize ideas from here to get more out of it. Just pick something you want to become better at and start using it in those easy games. You can always apply a status, play with space, and try different combinations of accepting, blocking, and offering. You can always play with how you're communicating, and you can observe what others are doing and learn from them. In other words, you can always be learning more!

Improv Manifesto

This is a starting off point. A beginning of an adventure of exploration. This book is not supposed to give you a bunch of rules to follow. If you try to eliminate your fear by covering it over with a bunch of rules, you'll lose out. You'll cover insecurity with the idea that you know the "right way to improvise." I don't think there is a "right way to make things up!" Once you have one way that's successful for you, continue finding more.

Here's a devastatingly obvious example. A woman came to a one-time, 90-minute class I held. She was a psychologist who'd just done an improv class series down in Portland. At one point in the class I broke everyone up into groups of 2 and had them practice blocking versus accepting. So, one person was supposed to say, "Yes, and…" and the other person said, "No, but." Just like we went over in chapter 3.

She interrupted as I was describing the game and said, "But I hate blocking! I don't want to do this! I love accepting. I love the Yes, and!"

If you're the astute person I know you are, you'll quickly notice whether she was blocking or accepting when she said that. She was **saying** she loved accepting… while she was **blocking!** I gently pointed out what was happening. The rest of the class got it, while I don't think she did and I didn't have time in that class to focus on her.

She had learned that you should only do "Yes, and…" It became a rule for her. Then, she forgot to pay attention to which she was doing. If she'd done the exercise in the class, she'd become more aware of when she was clocking and would start catching herself. (I was busy focusing on helping the people who wanted to learn, so I'm not certain of this, but I believe she refused to block her partners! She made them do it. She needed to be in control. She said no to saying no…)

This is extremely common. I've met people who've been doing improv for decades who don't apply what they learn to their lives. They actively do the opposite and the results show. The essence of improvisation isn't a set of rules. Fighting for the "right" rules and "right" ideas could be a lot of things, but I don't think it's improvisation. It's defending a comfort zone.

Rules are like training wheels. Imagine someone who criticized anyone who doesn't have training wheels on their bike! You could also think of rules like diapers. They're really useful at a young age to keep crap from getting everywhere. But, if you keep wearing them as an adult, your friends will start to complain about the stink!

I believe the essence of improvisation is learning to be in the moment. It's about letting go of control. It's letting go of fear. It's becoming aware of the little-known dynamics of human interaction. It's about courage and breaking out of your former limitations. It's about learning and becoming more open, more awake, and more alive.

If you're doing that, you're a world-class improviser in my book. And, since this is my book...

Thanks,
Chad Elliot
chad@seattleimprovclasses.com

The Beginning...

Enjoyably Bringing It All Together.

There's a boatload of useful information in this book. How do you tie this all together in a nice package with a bow and ribbon? After all, we need to be able to use it on the spur of the moment, right?

The first step is practicing each individual element. It's only through practice that it becomes automatic. As you focus on practicing one thing, you'll lose focus on something else. That's okay. The more you continue practicing, the more you'll discover that new behaviors and learnings become subconscious and you do them without thinking about it. That's the point at which you've really learned it in a useful way.

As you continue, you'll notice that it all fits together like a puzzle. Each piece fits with the others. You can't tell what a complete puzzle will look like when you're just looking at an individual piece. But, once you fit all of the pieces together with each other, it reveals an image that you didn't see when they were separate.

Let's say you want to do a scene. How can you bring all of what we've discussed together into a complete picture?

- First of all, you have to have the courage to get out there and do it (Chapter 7: Take Risks.)
- You begin confidently and enthusiastically to set yourself up for success (Chapter 2: Starting Powerfully.)
- You immediately create the platform of the story/scene (Chapter 4: Captivating Storytelling,) by creating who you are, where you are, and what you're doing (Chapter 5: Creating from Nothing.)
- It's easier to do that because you accept and build on anything that's offered (Chapter 3: Generating Ideas.)

- After you've set the platform, you tilt it and that changes the characters and status dynamics (Back to Chapter 4: Captivating Storytelling.)

Before you even go on stage:

- You've practiced being in the moment and simply continue that in front of an audience (Chapter 1: Be in the Moment.)
- As you're there, you maintain a strong stage presence (Chapter 6: Stage Presence.)
- If you get stuck, you can make an interesting blind verbal offer (Chapter 2: Starting Powerfully.) or a blind physical offer (Chapter 5: Creating from Nothing.) or accept and build on the ideas of others (Chapter 3: Creating Ideas.) or just be present and create a suspenseful silence (Chapter 6: Stage Presence.)

A Complete Improv Scene Transcript.

To show this all in action, I'm going to give you an example scene from my *Off-The-Cuff Podcast.* This episode had *The Dating Coach on Wheels*, Amin Lakhani, as the guest. If you'd like to listen to the episode before reading this scene, you can go to:

http://seattleimprovclasses.com/improvpodcast/otc-002-improv-dating-advice/

This was all entirely improvised, all that was agreed in advance is we'd do a scene with a tilt. Naturally, since it was recorded over VOIP, we couldn't even see each other. And yet, all the elements are here to explore. I've transcribed it as accurately as possible, including grammatical errors. (The mistakes in grammar are important because they help show the changes in status.) Here we go:

Chad: "Welcome. Come on in, Mr. Jenkins." (Vague offer of who they are and the context.)

Amin: "Oh, good to see you, James. Uh. I've been trying some of your strategies and I'm here for a little bit more." (Accepts and builds onto who they are and the context, creating some form of teacher/student relationship. Slight pausing and filler words help indicate his being lower status than the teacher.)

Chad: "Go ahead and tell me what's on your mind. Let yourself go. Relax." (Accepts and builds teacher/student relationship into patient/therapist. Begins giving instructions to indicate being higher status.)

Amin: "There's this person in my life, who, I just, I have all this rage toward this person." (Accepts and offers the patient's problem.)

Chad: "Is this person… you? Is this person you?" (Accepts problem and makes offer of therapeutic insight.)

Amin: "No, it's not me, James, it's not me." (Blocks therapeutic insight, but continues accepting therapeutic context.)

Chad: "Ah. Oh." (Accepts and is slightly lowered in status.)

Amin: "It's, uh, it's my wife!" (Offers new detail of problem.)

Chad: "Um hm. Um hm." (Accepts and responds in a therapist manner.)

Amin: "And, so, I just get so angry. I wake up and I think about how she didn't put the trash out. Or, how she didn't buy the milk for me. I just, I'm just so upset and angry with her." (Builds on therapeutic problem, fills out more aspects of his character.)

Chad: "Well, those are stupid things to be upset about! What's the matter with you?" (Accepts the facts that were added, blocks the importance of those facts. Insults the client and takes a much higher status position.)

Amin: "Uh, I, they, they, they really bother me, James, when I tell someone that I want them to do something and they don't do it." (Accepts confrontation by having character fight for importance of his offer/facts. By being in the defending position he's lower in status.)

Chad: "Ok. So, this doesn't sound like something worth dealing with. Do you have any other issues." (Accepts current relationship by blocking importance of client's problem and requesting better offers. Again, indicating higher status.)

Amin: "Any other issues..." (Accepting request and maintaining lower status.)

Chad: Talking over Amin and interrupting, "Other issues that will be worth my time. I want this to be worth my time as well as…

yours." (Conveying higher status by interrupting. Insulting Amin and raising self-importance by the emphasis on the worth of his time.)

Amin: "Ok." (Acceptance.)

Chad: "I mean, did you know that your wife is having an affair?" (Making an interesting offer and sets up tilt.)

Amin: "Yeah, I mean, I was going to get to that. That was… something else that gets me really upset. Is that she's been sleeping with this guys that she says is very nurturing and caring towards her." (Accepts and builds.)

Chad: "Yes, I absolutely, I mean, I'm sure he is." (Accepts and builds while continuing to set up the tilt.)

Amin: Taking on a more accusatory tone, "She says he's really good at listening to her." (Building and beginning to discover the implication of the coming tilt.)

Chad: "Absolutely. Absolutely. That's important in a relationship." (Continues building up to the tilt.)

Amin: "Yeah, and that really gets me going, James. Like, when I think about how she's talking to some other guy, and he's caring for her. And, I don't know what to do and I wake up..." (Continues building his worldview.)

Chad: "Well, you're not doing it! Well, you are not doing it!" (Interrupts and criticizes to lower client's status.)

Amin: "What am I supposed to do, James? If I can't do it for her..." (Accepts lower status. Asks advice with self deprecation contained in how he asks for it.)

Chad: "You need to let her go. You need to let her go. You need to let her go. You need to encourage her to be with this other man." (Gives advice, continuing higher status.)

Amin: "That sounds like… really… preemptive. I mean perhaps we can work through some things." (Character blocks advice. Slightly criticizes and so slightly lowers therapist's status.)

Chad: "You have obviously shown that you're not going to change. She's got this man in her life who's, who's, you know, a better listener, more intelligent, better looking. You should let her..." (Criticizes client and compliments clients rival, thereby lowering client and raising rival. Thoroughly hinting at tilt.)

Amin: "Better looking, hold on. Hold on here, James. How do you, how did you even know she was going through an affair? Have I told you about that? " (Interrupts and takes some control of the conversation, gradually raising his status. Accusatory questions that lower therapist's status. Character begins having realization of situation.)

Chad: "Look I feel there's some negative transference that's happening here, Bob. Let's go back to the main issue here. Um." (Character blocks accusation and implies problem in client. Attempts to take back control and regain high status.)

Amin: "Okay." (Accepts.)

Chad: "So, what are your feelings? So, what are your feelings?" (Takes back control and asks for offer related to feelings.)

Amin: "I'm feeling very angry! I don't know what to do about my wife cheating on this guy... cheating on me with this guy... who I don't even know anything about other than that he's a good listener." (Accepts and adds.)

Chad: Deep breath, then says, "Well, there's something I have, I should tell you, Bob. Um. I'm, I'm the one having an affair with your wife. " (Pause to create tension. Speaks in sentence broken with ums and repetition to start lowering status. Makes full revelation of tilt. No longer just a therapist/client relationship. Now relationship is one of a therapist who is having an affair with the client's wife and the client/husband who has just found out.)

Long pause building tension...

Amin: "I don't even know what to say right now. (Pause.) Are you kidding me!" (Accepts and gives reaction of disbelief by asking for confirmation.)

Chad: "That's good..." (Accepts and tries to regain higher status.)

Amin: "How long has that been going on?!" (Interrupts. Accepts new knowledge. Takes control by requesting offer of additional details. Taking higher status.)

Chad: "It's been going on since you started coming here. So, for about 6 months. Sooo, look! Like I..." (Accepts and gives offer of information. Fulfilling requests made of him continues lowering his status.)

Amin: "James. Are you serious? This entire time! You've been seeing my wife?" (Accepts and adds response of anger.)

Chad: "Woh! Woh! Woh! Woh! Woh! Woh!" (Accepts anger and begins blind offer of what the client is physically doing.)

Amin: "That's not okay... James!" (Gives condemnation, lowering therapist's status further. His sentences are getting shorter, while the therapist's sentences are getting longer. Again, an indication of the change in power dynamics.)

Chad: "Put that down! Put that down! Put that down and sit back down..." (Makes blind offer more clear by indicating client is holding something dangerous.)

Amin: "I will stab you with this, if you do not let go of my wife..." (Accepts blind offer and fills in with offer of something that stabs, probably knife or scissors. Makes threat. Taking higher status even more fully.)

Chad: "Woh! Woh! I tell ya what, I tell ya what, we'll talk about it. Maybe you are the better man! Maybe you are the better man, I don't know?" (Repeating parts of sentence, indicating fear and lowering of power. Trying to make a deal. Directly indicates possibility that the client is actually better than him.)

Amin: "That sounds more like what I want to hear, James. Tell me more about why I'm the better man." (Accepting and indicating approval - and therefore the higher position of being judge of what is acceptable. Makes demand of more offers in line with what satisfies him. He's clearly in the superior position.)

Chad: "Because, because you are an incredibly charming person. You... have... incredible insight into people! And that, and that you notice things about people that nobody else notices. And, and, your wife told me that when she still loved you, that she uh, I mean that one of the things she loved about you was that you're just so, uh, that you notice things about her that, uh, that other people didn't notice!?" (Does as ordered, demonstrating that client has power and therapist now does as told.. Gives compliments, attempting to raise client directly. Speaks in fragments, with ums and ahs. Obviously trying to say what will please the client.)

Amin: Talking over each other, "Yeah. Yeah." (Accepts.)

Chad: Talking over each other, "So go ahead calm down, put it down, put it down." (Tries to take back control and regain the previous power dynamic.)

Amin: "Yeah, I guess, wait! Tell me when you're going to end it!" (Blocks attempt at control and makes another demand.)

Chad: "Come on. I mean, she, uh, obviously loves, uh, me, uh, more than she loves… you!" (Attempts to block and resists fulfilling demand. Speaks in fragments while insulting the client, indicating lower status behaviorally, while indicating higher status in actual words.)

Amin: Talking over each other, "Uh. I don't know what to do!" (Accepts and adds internal conflict about further action.)

Chad: Talking over each other, "Whoa! Step back! Step back!" (Makes offer that client is moving toward him.)

Amin: "I'm just going to..." (Accepts.)

Chad: "No, Bob! AHHH! Oh, jeez! " (Offers that he's been hurt.)

Amin: "I think I'm going to just end it all." (Accepts and makes offer of further action.)

Chad: "Please, please don't do that again." (Accepts and pleads for life.)

Amin: "If she can't be with me, then she definitely doesn't deserve to be with you." (Accepts and builds on violence theme.)

Chad: "AHH!" (Indicates acceptance of attack by making sound of being mortally wounded. Laser sound added later for fun. Bob, the client, ends up clearly in the more powerful and James, the therapist, in the weaker position. A complete reversal from the start of the scene.)

Amin: "Goodbye, James!" (Final words indicating end of scene.)

In examining this, you can see some clear aspects of what happened.

1. At the start, we **created the platform.** We quickly established who we were, where we were, and our relationship to each other. In other words. That relationship was both defined through titles (patient/therapist,) and status (high/low.)

2. **A tilt to the relationship was introduced,** gradually. Amin didn't know what the tilt was going to be, so I made hints until he caught on. I could have told him straight out without any hinting, and it would have had a different feel.

3. After the tilt was clearly made, the person surprised by the tilt **responded strongly.**

4. Then, the **relationship dynamics changed.** The person who was on top moved to the bottom, and vice versa. We made **an effort to handle the new problems** and handle the new shift in dynamics.

5. There was an eventual **clear resolution.**

To summarize another way, this was a scene with a clear storyline. It was a Platform/Tilt type of storyline and it had a clear Status relationship and final Reversal of Status.

If you want to be able to do this consistently and reliably, it demonstrates the minimum skills you must have to make it happen.

- You need to accept and build on offers.
- You need to create a status for your character.
- You need to create a strong tilt and respond intensely.
- You need to utilize the tilt to drive the story forward.
- You need to create status change to show character development and find a resolution.

If you simply focus on doing that, you can create a compelling scene. That is by no means the only way to do it, but it's one very effective way. All of the tools and skills we've discussed throughout the book contribute to being able to do this successfully. The more you develop each skill, the more you'll find fun, new ways to pull things together. It will become a playground for your creativity and exploration. As you practice these skills in this playful context, you'll enjoy how quickly you discover it effortlessly expanding into the other areas of your life. You can enjoy your life story beautifully unfolding before your eyes in new and surprising directions.

Learn More with Chad

I'm the owner of Seattle Improv Classes and I teach classes in improv, creativity, storytelling, and communication. I also do coaching calls in a way that's very personalized to your needs. In fact, I'm the first person in the world to make one-on-one coaching an integral part of improv training. I have a rich and diverse background in teaching and coaching. What I really do is assist you in learning about yourself, the world, and how you can get a lot more of what you want in your life. And, I make sure we have a lot of fun doing it!

If you're interested in taking my classes, coaching with me, or having me come into your organization to lead a powerful "funshop," you can email me at chad@seattleimprovclasses.com Visit SeattleImprovClasses.com Or, call 425-270-1989. I have a special coaching package available for readers of this book. Just send me an email or call for more info.

Made in the USA
Columbia, SC
01 September 2017